The Kentucky Bourbon Cookbook

The

KENTUCKY
BOURBON
COOKBOOK

Albert W. A. Schmid

FOREWORD BY CHEF DEAN FEARING

THE UNIVERSITY PRESS OF KENTUCKY

Photographs provided by Kriech-Higdon Photography

Scholarly publisher for the Commonwealth, serving Bellarmine University, Berea College, Centre
College of Kentucky, Eastern Kentucky University, The Filson Historical Society, Georgetown College,
Kentucky Historical Society, Kentucky State University, Morehead State University, Murray State
University, Northern Kentucky University, Transylvania University, University of Kentucky, University
of Louisville, and Western Kentucky University.

Editorial and Sales Offices: The University Press of Kentucky
663 South Limestone Street, Lexington, Kentucky 40508-4008

www.kentuckypress.com

14 13 12 11 10   5 4 3 2 1

Library of Congress Cataloging-in-Publication Data
Schmid, Albert W. A.
  The Kentucky bourbon cookbook / Albert W. A. Schmid.
    p. cm.
  Includes bibliographical references and index.
  ISBN 978-0-8131-2579-4 (hardcover : alk. paper)
  1. Cookery (Whiskey) 2. Cocktails. 3. Cookery, American—Southern style. I. Title.
  TX726.S365 2010
  641.6'25—dc22   2009045877

Manufactured in Canada.

 Member of the Association of American University Presses

TO MY FATHER, the Rev. Dr. Thomas Schmid, because you love bourbon and my mother.

TO MY MOTHER, Elizabeth Schmid, because you love fine cuisine and my father.

ENJOY YOUR RETIREMENT!

CONTENTS

FOREWORD

ALTHOUGH I HAVE MADE TEXAS my home since arriving in Dallas in 1979, I am proud to be from Kentucky. I was born in Ashland, in the far eastern part of the state, where my first food memories are of the simple but perfectly seasoned cooking of my grandmothers. I still use and treasure their recipes to this day, and much of my culinary inspiration can be traced to their early influence. Later, my father ran hotels in Louisville and elsewhere. He encouraged my interest in food and taught me valuable lessons in southern hospitality that have shaped my career as a chef and owner of my own restaurant.

To me, Kentucky means family, history, Bluegrass music, horses, corn bread and biscuits, country ham, barbecue, and bourbon. And oh Lordy, do I love a glass of good bourbon. I also love cooking with bourbon, as my family, friends, and everyone else who has tasted my cooking over the years will tell you.

There has never been a better time for a cookbook that explores the use of bourbon in cooking. People everywhere are interested in fine bourbon, fine cooking, and food and beverage pairing. I applaud Chef Albert Schmid for putting together this valuable collection of bourbon history, lore, and recipes, including my own recipes for Kentucky Bourbon–Pecan Crème Brûlée with Chocolate Sauce (pp. 38–39) and Kentucky Chocolate Bourbon Pecan Pie (pp. 54–55). I hope you enjoy this taste of my childhood home, Kentucky.

DEAN FEARING
CHEF/PARTNER, FEARING'S RESTAURANT
DALLAS, TEXAS

ACKNOWLEDGMENTS

MANY PEOPLE CONTRIBUTED to the completion of this book. First of all, I want to thank my wife Kimberly and my sons Thomas and Michael, as well as my Kentucky parents, Richard and Carol Dunn, for their love and support. And I thank my grandfather the Rev. Richard Wheatcroft for his love and support during my entire life.

Thanks are also due to the following people for their direct or indirect support of this project.

My sisters, my brother, and their spouses, Gretchen, Tiffany, Rachel, Justin, Bennett, Anna, Shane, and John: For your love and support.

The late Kerry Sommerville, who died at the tender age of fifty-one: You were both a mentor and a lover of fine food and bourbon. I know you would have loved this compilation of recipes combining the two. Thank you for encouraging the early stages of the project. You were a good friend, a fine boss, and an excellent writer, and you are missed.

Chris Morris, Master Distiller and master teacher: Thank you for helping me understand the complexities of bourbon.

Adam Segar, good friend and former colleague: Thank you for your scholarship on the subject of wines and spirits (especially bourbon). You always raise the bar (pun intended).

Quentin and Tresa Moser, my good friends: Thank you for your appreciation of everything liquid and for pushing me to push myself to a new level of understanding of beverage.

Scot Duvall: Thank you for your friendly counsel.

Lois Crum: Thank you for copyediting this book.

Sarah Nichter: Thanks for being my friend and for copyediting an early version of this book.

Brian and Angie Clute, my good friends: Thank you for your ear and your support.

Chef Thomas Hickey, the Director of the National Center for Hospitality Studies at Sullivan University: Thanks for your mentorship and for allowing me to write.

Edward "Jon" Bjornson, my new friend: Thank you for your leadership, support, and understanding.

Chef Anne Sandhu, my good friend and fellow chef: Thank you for your friendship and support.

Dawn McGiffen, my good friend: Thank you for your support and advice.

Gaby Berliner, my office neighbor and friend: I appreciate your support.

Abdeljalil "Eddie" Maamry, my good friend and fellow beverage lover: Thank you for all your support and your friendship.

Chef David Dodd, Chef Alan Akmon, Chef Derek Spendlove, and Chef Kimberly Jones: Thank you for chairing the programs at Sullivan University's National Center for Hospitality Studies; and thank you for your leadership and mentorship.

Chancellor A.R. Sullivan: Thank you for your support of my writing and for leading the great university where I work.

President Glenn Sullivan: Thank you for your support of my writing, for your leadership, for your copyediting of this text, and for your love of Kentucky's state beverage, bourbon. Also, thank you for sponsoring the photo shoot and the food styling for this book.

Laura Sutton: Thank you for your thoughts and ideas on my writing and for your support of this project.

The Winston's staff, including Kevin O'Nions, Sara Abshire, John Lowry, Megan Cantryman, Jordon Kharizana, Matt Flink, Chef John Castro, and Chef Aaron Adams: Thank you for your help and support the day of the photo shoot for this book.

My students, including Josh Wise (who acted as my sous chef for the photo shoot), Seannesha Bussell, Avalon Sutherland, Carolynn Siavaila, Barry Queen, Jimi Weis, Oliver Miller, Erin Polley, TJ Stults, Amanda Mengedont, Duncan Williams, Hilary Lesch, Lauren Tabereaux, Karen Lheureau, Jared Brosmer, Leslie Irvin, Marcia Botner, Mark Garson, Gage Campbell, Sergey Katz, and Armonte Yarbrough: Thank you for your help preparing food for the photo shoot.

Andrea Pridham: Thank you for allowing us space on Farmington Historic Plantation for the photo shoot.

Finally, I would like to thank the following musical artists, whose music I listened to while writing this book: Jeff Healey and his band, Isaac Hayes, Darius Rucker, The Neville Brothers, and the Kentucky natives Eddie Montgomery and Troy Gentry who make up the duo Montgomery Gentry.

INTRODUCTION

I LOVE FOOD AND I LOVE BOURBON. My first exposure to fine cuisine and bourbon occurred when I was a student at the McDonogh 15 elementary school. There, as I began learning the three Rs, I also began studying food and gastronomy. Although I didn't know it at the time, it was one of the best places in the world for such study—the French Quarter in New Orleans. My father and mother moved to "the Big Easy" so my father could become pastor of the Eastminster Presbyterian Church in New Orleans East. Every day my parents would drive me across town to my school in the French Quarter. On the way I took in the culture and the smells of New Orleans. Some mornings we would stop at Café du Monde, across from Jackson Square, for beignets and café au lait (I always had chocolate milk) before we reached my school, which was on St. Phillips Street between Royal and Bourbon. I was not the only student who attended class with confectioners' sugar on his shirt.

McDonogh 15 was a progressive school, where the teachers believed students would learn as much from their environment as they did in the classroom. So a lot of "class" time was spent touring the French Quarter. My senses were tantalized, and the aromas, the sights, and the flavors I experienced on these field trips influence me to this day. New Orleans is where I developed my love for the tangible pleasures of life. When my parents would pick me up in the afternoon, we might stop on St. Ann's Street for red beans and rice at Buster Holmes, or get a po' boy at one of the many shops that sold seafood subway-style sandwiches with crusty French bread, or visit the Central Grocery for a muffuletta. I also became aware of the fine cuisine of New Orleans: the food served at the Empire restaurant owned by the Brennan family, at K-Paul's, at LaRuth's, at Antoine's, and at Arnaud's. The city of New Orleans and its citizens love food as much as they love life, and for some of them food is life.

I remember one night when my father sat in his chair holding a glass shallowly filled with a dark amber liquid and ice. He sipped the beverage. I asked if I could taste it, but he said no; it was an "adult drink." He did allow me a sniff, though. It was bourbon, and I was so overwhelmed by the smell of alcohol that I missed the caramel, vanilla, licorice, and sweet oak that my father enjoyed. Over the years I heard my father quote the Bible, where it says "Man cannot live on bread alone." I knew that beverage was essential to human life. A person can live longer without bread than without beverage. I must admit that my father was not referring to bourbon from his pulpit. But for some, especially in Kentucky, beverage, and more specifically bourbon, is life (and for some it is their livelihood).

When I became an adult, I thought I had to avoid bourbon because I was allergic to corn, a primary bourbon ingredient. It was at an International Association of Culinary Professionals (IACP) conference in San Diego in 2002 that I learned otherwise. Lincoln Henderson, the master distiller for Brown-Forman at the time, presented at the conference I was attending, and I had the pleasure of dining with him and my friends Adam Segar and Chris Morris. Lincoln bought a round of bourbon for the table, but I declined, mentioning my allergy to corn, and asked if mine could be a Scotch, which is made primarily from barley. As if Warren Buffet was about to speak about the economy or investments, the table became silent. Lincoln explained that what I was allergic to was lost in the distillation process. That evening I was converted from Scotch to bourbon.

Another vital lesson related to the development of this book was learned at the 2008 meeting of the IACP in New Orleans. While I was there, Dickie Brennan's Bourbon House hosted Master Distiller Harlen Wheatley from the Buffalo Trace Distillery for a bourbon pairing dinner. The bourbon was supplied by the distillery from my home state, and the food was prepared by Chef Darin Nesbit in what used to be my hometown. It was a five course meal:

FIRST COURSE

Bacon Pastrami–Wrapped Shrimp with
Toasted Ancho Chili Stone Grits and Candied Lemon,
paired with Buffalo Trace

SECOND COURSE

Brown Sugar–Cured Diver Scallops with
Chili-Pecan Dressing and Chicory Vinaigrette,
paired with Buffalo Trace

COUP DU MILIEU

Pappy Van Winkle 20 year

THIRD COURSE

Buffalo Osso Bucco with Molasses Sweet Potatoes,
Caramelized Peaches, Bourbon Demi-Glacé, and Caramel "Hay,"
paired with Sazerac Rye

DESSERT

Dark Chocolate Bread Pudding Soufflé with Bourbon Sauce,
paired with George T. Stagg

Before I ate this meal, I had believed that bourbon was not the best beverage to pair with food. I considered bourbon an "after-dinner drink," but this meal proved to me that bourbon could pair excellently with food. I found that to stand up to the intense flavor of bourbon, the food itself has to be full-bodied. Only those foods with a specific flavor profile pair well and accept bourbon into a recipe without damaging or overpowering the other components of the dish. For example, in the second course, the reason the scallops work with the bourbon pairing is the addition of the brown sugar, the chili-pecan dressing, and the chicory vinaigrette. The additions to the seafood pump up the flavor of the dish and intensify what would otherwise be a light-bodied dish. At the end of the meal, my palate was overwhelmed from all the rich food and beverage. I walked down Bourbon Street and through the French Quarter back to my hotel satisfied with the knowledge that bourbon and food worked well together. (See the appendix for recipes for the dishes I was served at Dickie Brennan's Bourbon House.)

As I researched recipes with bourbon, I noticed that with very few exceptions bourbon is utilized only in southern cooking or by southern expatriates. Not every regional cuisine uses bourbon in its food. In New Orleans, for example, although the city has a connection to bourbon, Cajun and Creole cuisines use very little bourbon. However, you might find bourbon in a dessert whiskey sauce. In Kentucky cuisine you might find more use of bourbon, but it is by no means a staple, nor is it a main component in any dish. Bourbon is a secondary ingredient used in small ratios to flavor food. For these reasons, there are not many cookbooks that feature recipes with bourbon, and those that do exist tend to duplicate recipes from other books. People have different palates, and there are many types of bourbon on the market. The recipes in this book should be made with whichever bourbon you like best, maximizing your enjoyment of the dishes you create.

Most cookbooks are set up by courses: appetizers, entrées, side dishes, and desserts. But after chapter 1, which is devoted to beverages, this cookbook is organized by seasons: winter, spring, summer, and fall. In some cases the food in the recipes is seasonal, grown only at certain times of the year, and in others the recipe itself is seasonal, not commonly prepared during the other seasons. For example, "Spring" is filled with recipes good for the Kentucky Derby and Easter, while "Winter" features recipes that are best served during the Christmas holiday. "Summer" has grilled items that invoke hot summer days in the backyard with a grill, and "Fall" includes recipes for Thanksgiving.

I hope that, beyond re-creating the treats in the following pages, the home cook and the professional chef alike can use the recipes for inspiration to create new dishes that incorporate bourbon. The book can serve as a lesson both on the flavor profiles that pair and improve with bourbon and on what works when you add bourbon to recipes from many masters of the kitchen.

CHAPTER ONE

BEVERAGES

Recipes for All Seasons

B ourbon is a kind of whiskey. *Whisk(e)y* is a word spelled two ways, with and without the *e*. The term is an English word of Celtic origin that comes from "uisce beatha" in Gaelic and "usice beatha" in Irish and is equivalent to "eau de vie" in French or "aqua vitae" in Latin. All of those terms mean "the water of life."[1] How someone spells *whisk(e)y* has a lot to do with where the beverage is made, where the person's family comes from, and what tradition he or she is trying to follow. For example, there is Scotch whisky and Irish whiskey. As Scots moved from their homeland to Nova Scotia (New Scotland), they brought with them the technology to make distilled beverage, and the spelling *whisky* came along too; so all Canadian whisky is spelled without the *e*. In the United States, some distilleries produce whiskey and others produce whisky. Again, the family origin of the whisk(e)y maker is suggested. This explains why Maker's Mark and Old Forester are whisky, while Jim Beam and Old Rip Van Winkle are whiskey. In any case, these four whiskeys are all bourbon. There are many other bourbon labels, the vast majority of them made in Kentucky, but technically bourbon can be made outside of the Bluegrass state as well.

Most people believe a Baptist minister, the Reverend Elijah Craig, was the first person to distill bourbon, circa 1789. It was a very convenient legend for the forces trying to repeal Prohibition (the Eighteenth Amendment to the U.S. Constitution, also known as the Volstead Act). After all, how bad can bourbon be if it was invented by a Baptist minister? Prohibition lasted from 1920 to 1933 and was ended by the Twenty-first Amendment. The truth is that no one knows who invented bourbon. Some of the favorite candidates include Evan Williams, James Ritchie, and Wattie Boone (Daniel's cousin). The legend of bourbon became reality in 1964 when bourbon was officially named America's native spirit by the U.S. Congress. Congress decreed that bourbon could be made only in the United States and that whiskey made in the United States must meet certain criteria in order to be labeled "bourbon."[2] The requirements for bourbon are these:

- Bourbon must be made from at least 51 percent corn mixed with barley and with rye or wheat or both. Many times bourbon has an even higher percentage of corn, but it never exceeds 79 percent of the mash. (When the percentage of mash reaches 80%, the beverage becomes corn whiskey.)
- Bourbon must be aged for at least two years in charred new oak barrels. If it is aged less than four years, a statement of age must be placed on the label.
- Only pure water may be added to bourbon.
- Bourbon must not exceed 160 proof off the still or 125 proof going into the barrel.

Before the Revolutionary War, in the Colonies, whiskey was made from rye. But rye does not grow very well in the southern states, so as whiskey-making moved south, it was necessary to find a new grain to use. The introduction of corn as the major ingredient also changed the flavor profile of whiskey. When the Colonies became the United States of America, the newly formed government was cash poor, having racked up massive debts to finance the war with Great Britain. Alexander Hamilton, the new secretary of the treasury, proposed that Congress impose a tax on whiskey to help retire the debt.[3] This tax was not popular with the farmers who grew corn for a living, because many farmers were distilling their corn into whiskey for ease of transport to the local market, where the whiskey could serve as a substitute for cash.[4] In fact, during this time whiskey was the most stable currency in the United States and the most versatile, since each state printed its own currency and in some cases one state did not recognize the currency from other states. In 1794, when tax collectors pressed the farmers to pay the tax, seventeen hundred insurgent farmers broke into open revolt. President George Washington called up between thirteen thousand and fifteen thousand militia troops from Virginia, Maryland, New Jersey, and Pennsylvania to put down the rebellion.[5] Even though no shots were fired, this became the first time a commander-in-chief personally led troops into a potential battle. After the Whiskey Rebellion, the federal government offered settlers sixty acres of land west of the Alleghenies, with the provision that they make a permanent home and grow corn. Many farmers moved west to Bourbon County, Kentucky, where they made whiskey from the native grain.[6] Much of this whiskey was stored in barrels stamped "BOURBON" and shipped down the Ohio River to the Mississippi River and on to New Orleans.[7] Eventually, this new whiskey claimed the name of the county in which it was pioneered. An alternative story of how bourbon got its name is that Americans named this whiskey after the French royal family the Bourbons, to honor them for their help during the Revolutionary War and to distinguish it from the whiskey that came from the British Empire. Bourbon is the most regulated whiskey in the world and one of the most regulated spirits, a fact that seems contrary to the American spirit of freedom and limited regulation.[8] Nevertheless, bourbon is exclusively American.

Bourbon has become an American tradition. It goes with any holiday or other occasion when you might want to serve a high-quality whiskey. Bourbon can be served straight up (neat) in a shot glass or an Old Fashioned glass, over ice (on the rocks), with water (bourbon and branch), or mixed with soda water or some other mixer such as cola. Bourbon can also serve as the base for many mixed drinks. Whiskey complements many foods, such as apples, bacon, beef, cheese (especially blue cheese), grilled seafood or grilled chicken, fried chicken, figs, dried fruit, game, wild mushrooms (morels), roasted pork, smoked salmon, shellfish, oysters, venison, and chocolate desserts.[9] Bourbon is also an ingredient in many recipes. Why shouldn't it be? At culinary schools all over the nation, instructors teach their students that to have a high-quality finished product, a chef must start with ingredients of the highest quality. Bourbon is the highest-quality whiskey in the world. This statement is based on the production standards of bourbon; remember, nothing is added to bourbon except pure water. All the other whiskeys may have caramel coloring added before bottling. Also, because of bourbon's sweet-spicy flavor, it complements food in a way that many other whiskeys do not. For example, the peat in Scotch and some Irish whiskeys make these whiskeys less food friendly.

Perhaps one of the oldest recipes that contains Bourbon is this one:[10]

THE MOST FAMOUS OF ALL KENTUCKY BREAKFASTS

1 steak
1 quart bourbon whiskey
1 man (you can substitute a woman)
1 dog

The man throws the steak to the dog and drinks the bourbon.

This is an old joke, but it is true that many years ago hard liquors were consumed at breakfast time. In fact a "cock tail" was originally a morning drink.[11]

Bourbon is in its most common state in the following recipes.

PRESBYTERIAN

The Presbyterian was considered a woman's drink in the 1950s and 1960s, because at that time men consumed straight whiskey. This drink is light and refreshing and very easy to make. Stirring is not necessary, since the carbonation will automatically "stir" the ingredients together if the directions are followed. I found a similar drink in *The Essential Cocktail*, by Dale DeGroff, who is known as the King of Cocktails.[12]

Ice
3 tablespoons Kentucky bourbon
¼ cup club soda
¼ cup ginger ale
Lemon peel

Fill a highball glass with ice and pour the bourbon over the ice. Add the club soda and ginger ale. Twist the lemon peel, releasing the oil in the peel. Rub the peel around the rim of the glass and place the peel in the glass.

SEELBACH COCKTAIL

If Dale DeGroff is the king of cocktails, my friend Adam Seger is a grand duke. Seger and his cocktail recipes regularly appear in national magazines, and he has worked with and has become one of the who's whos in the restaurant industry. He is coauthor of the forthcoming book *Whet: Drink Like You Eat*. This recipe and the next are from him.

> 2 tablespoons Kentucky bourbon
> 1 tablespoon Cointreau
> 7 dashes Angostura bitters
> 7 dashes Peychaud Bitters
> ½ cup plus 2 tablespoons champagne
> Orange twist

Pour the bourbon, Cointreau, and bitters into a champagne flute and stir. Pour the champagne into the flute and stir again. Garnish with an orange twist.

BLUEGRASS BREAKFAST

Here is an example of a "breakfast" drink from Seger. For this drink he combines several items with bourbon that people associate with breakfast. This drink uses the process of "muddling" fruit to extract the juice and flavor from the fruit for the drink. Muddling is crushing the fruit with a small bat-shaped tool. The back of a spoon will work if you don't have a muddler.

> ¼ cup fresh blueberries
> Half a lemon, sliced
> 6-inch sprig of fresh rosemary
> Ice
> ¼ cup Kentucky bourbon
> 1 tablespoon maple syrup

In a 16-ounce glass (or Boston shaker), place the blueberries, lemon, and rosemary. Muddle these ingredients until juicy. Add ice, bourbon, and maple syrup. Shake until cold and then strain into a chilled cocktail glass. Garnish by putting on the edge of the glass a blueberry with a tiny sprig of rosemary sticking out.

KENTUCKY WHISKEY (BOURBON) TODDY

Not all whiskey made in Kentucky is bourbon. As already discussed, a whiskey must follow very specific regulations to be considered bourbon. A slight deviation from these regulations, such as aging the spirit in used (not new) oak barrels, disqualifies it. A toddy is a sweetened alcoholic drink that is usually served warm. This recipe, based on a drink from Marion Flexner's classic *Out of Kentucky Kitchens*, originally featured Kentucky whiskey but is enjoyed here with bourbon.[13]

½ teaspoon sugar
1 tablespoon tap water
   Crushed ice
¼ cup Kentucky bourbon

Mix the sugar and water in an Old Fashioned glass and fill with crushed ice. Add the bourbon, stir until chilled, and serve. For a warm toddy, carefully warm the water, bourbon, and sugar in a pot on the stove until it reaches 110 degrees or until lukewarm.

NEW ORLEANS COCKTAIL

The city of New Orleans helped bourbon claim its name. Therefore, it is fitting that the Big Easy be honored with a cocktail based on bourbon. In 1806, cocktails were defined by an editor of the newspaper *Balance and Columbian Repository* in Hudson, New York, as "stimulating liquor composed of spirits of any kind, sugar, water, and bitters." I found a similar recipe in *The New Orleans Bartender* by Sean Koskela.[14]

3 tablespoons Kentucky bourbon
1 tablespoon Pernod
1 dash Peychaud Bitters
1 dash Angostura bitters
1 dash anisette
   Simple syrup
   Cracked ice
   Lemon peel twist

Place the bourbon, Pernod, the two types of bitters, anisette, simple syrup (to taste), and cracked ice in a Boston shaker. Shake well and strain into a cocktail glass. Twist the lemon peel above the glass and place the peel in the glass.

SAZERAC

Another drink that helped form the persona of New Orleans is the Sazerac. The Sazerac was originally made with rye, but today most are made with bourbon. This drink is so important to New Orleans that the Louisiana Legislature has more than once considered a resolution to recognize the Sazerac as the official drink of New Orleans (each time the resolution has failed to pass).

	Pernod
1	sugar cube or 1 teaspoon superfine sugar
3	dashes bitters
	Strip of orange zest
	Strip of lemon zest
	Crushed ice
¼	cup Kentucky bourbon

Pour into an Old Fashioned glass enough Pernod to coat the bottom and sides. (The remainder of the Pernod may be discarded or used to make a second drink.) Drop the sugar cube into the glass. Drip the bitters onto the sugar cube and crush the cube with the back of a spoon. Rub the lemon and orange zest around the rim of the glass and deposit the zests in the glass. Add the crushed ice to fill the glass to ⅔ full. Pour the bourbon in.

NIXON

The Nixon was created by Joe Gilmore, the head bartender at the Savoy Hotel's American bar, to honor Richard M. Nixon's trip to Great Britain in the first year of his presidency. Gilmore created other drinks to commemorate royals, including Queen Elizabeth II and Charles, the Prince of Wales. He also invented a drink for President Harry S. Truman (see the Missouri Mule recipe, next) and for Neil Armstrong's "one small step" on the moon. Only the Nixon and the Missouri Mule are made with bourbon.

2 tablespoons Kentucky bourbon
2 tablespoons sloe gin
2 dashes peach bitters
  Ice
  Slice of fresh peach
  Cherry

Add the bourbon, sloe gin, and peach bitters to a Boston shaker filled with ice. Stir and strain these ingredients into an ice-filled cocktail glass. Garnish with the slice of peach and cherry.

MISSOURI MULE

The Missouri Mule was created by Joe Gilmore to honor President Harry S. Truman and Missouri, Truman's home state. Before he became president, Truman was the third vice president who served with Franklin D. Roosevelt, and one of the things Truman and Roosevelt (and Roosevelt's first vice president, John Nance "Cactus Jack" Garner IV) had in common was their love for bourbon.[15] The mule is Missouri's state animal.

2 tablespoons Kentucky bourbon
2 tablespoons applejack
2 tablespoons lemon juice
1 tablespoon Campari
1 tablespoon Cointreau
  Ice

Pour the bourbon, applejack, lemon juice, Campari, and Cointreau into a Boston shaker filled with ice. Shake until cold and strain into a cocktail glass.

GENERAL WASHINGTON'S GROG

The first president of the United States, George Washington, owned a brewery and a distillery at Mount Vernon. The Mount Vernon distillery, recently reopened, distills both rye and bourbon. Could this recipe be the secret to the survival of General Washington and his troops at Valley Forge?[16] "Old Grog" was the nickname of Admiral Edward Vernon, the man who lent his last name to the Washington residence, and because Admiral Vernon required his sailors to drink a mixture of rum and water every day to ward off scurvy, his sailors named the drink grog after him. The U.S. Navy continued the practice of serving grog to sailors until September 1, 1862.

- ½ cup plus 2 tablespoons water
- 2 tablespoons Madeira
- ¼ cup Kentucky bourbon
- 1 teaspoon brown sugar
- 1 whole clove
- 1 cinnamon stick
- 1 tablespoon butter

Bring the water to a boil. Add the Madeira, bourbon, brown sugar, clove, and cinnamon stick to the water and continue heating. When the grog is hot, remove it from the heat. Remove and reserve the cinnamon stick. Place the butter in a mug, and add the hot grog to the mug. Garnish with the cinnamon stick.

KENTUCKY BOURBON MANHATTAN

According to legend, the original Manhattan cocktail was created at the behest of Lady Randolph (Jennie Jerome) Churchill, the mother of Sir Winston Churchill, to honor newly elected New York governor Samuel J. Tilden. Tilden was a "Bourbon Democrat," a conservative or "classical liberal" member of the Democratic Party. This meant he believed in limited government. Even though the term *Bourbon Democrat* lost its meaning in popular culture around the turn of the twentieth century, it is very fitting that Tilden be honored with a drink that refers to New York and features an American whiskey (originally any American whiskey was used to make the Manhattan cocktail). David Wondrich, author of *Imbibe!* recently questioned this cocktail legend, pointing out that Lady Jennie was in England giving birth to Sir Winston at the time she supposedly asked to have Tilden honored.[17]

When making a Manhattan, consider what vermouth you want to use. Vermouth is a fortified, spiced wine that comes in three styles: extra dry, white, and sweet (which is red). As a flavorful component in this cocktail, the choice of vermouths makes the difference between a dry and a sweet Manhattan. This recipe is based on one found in *The Craft of the Cocktail*, by Dale DeGroff.[18]

¼ cup Kentucky bourbon
2 tablespoons sweet vermouth
1 dash Angostura bitters
1 dash Peychaud bitters
    Ice
1 cherry

Add the bourbon, vermouth, and bitters to a Boston shaker containing lots of ice. Shake until the ingredients are chilled, then strain into a cocktail glass. Garnish by dropping the cherry to the bottom of the glass.

WALDORF COCKTAIL

The Waldorf cocktail brings to mind the iconic New York Waldorf-Astoria Hotel, which started as two separate hotels, the Waldorf Hotel (finished in 1893) and the Astoria Hotel (finished in 1897). They were built by competing cousins William Waldorf Astor and John Jacob Astor IV. John's father, William Backhouse Astor Jr., owned the 1876 winner of the Kentucky Derby, Vagrant. I found this recipe in *Cocktail Classics*, by David Biggs.[19]

Crushed ice
¼ cup Kentucky bourbon
2 tablespoons Pernod
2 tablespoons sweet vermouth
1 dash Angostura bitters

Place the crushed ice in a cocktail shaker. Add the bourbon, Pernod, vermouth, and bitters. Stir well and strain into a cocktail glass.

OLD FASHIONED BOURBON COCKTAIL

The idea that the Old Fashioned whiskey cocktail was created at the Pendennis Club in Louisville, Kentucky, has been spread far and wide. Recently author David Wondrich dispelled this myth when he discovered a clear reference to the "Old Fashioned" in a 1869 issue of the Chicago Tribune.[20] (The Pendennis Club was not founded until 1881.) Even though the true origin of this cocktail is not known, the Old Fashioned is an adaptation from another cocktail, perhaps the whiskey cobbler or the whiskey cocktail, and led to other adaptations such as the mint julep. Some older recipes for the Old Fashioned call for a sprig of mint and were called "Juleps made the Old Fashioned Way."[21] No matter where the Old Fashioned whiskey cocktail originated, the people of Kentucky were kind enough to adopt this drink and give it a permanent home at the Pendennis Club. Thus, no matter where in the world the Old Fashioned whiskey cocktail is served, its true home is among the bluegrass. This recipe is based on one from another Wondrich book, *Esquire Drinks*.[22]

½ teaspoon sugar (or one sugar cube)
   2 to 3 dashes Angostura bitters
1 splash water
1 slice orange
1 cherry
   Ice
¼ cup plus 1 tablespoon Kentucky bourbon

Mix the sugar, bitters, and water in an Old Fashioned glass. Add the orange slice and the cherry and muddle. Add ice to the glass to fill. Add the bourbon in three equal portions, stirring after each addition.

TROPICAL ITCH

The British were the first westerners to happen upon the chain of islands known today as the state of Hawaii, and they named the islands for the First Lord of the Admiralty, Lord John Montagu, 4th Earl of Sandwich. Lord Sandwich was an avid gambler who did not want to leave the poker table, so he instructed his servants to place leftover roast beef between two slices of bread. In this way the earl could continue to gamble while he ate, and he didn't dirty his fingers. Even though most tourists order the Mai Tai when vacationing in Hawaii, another option is the Tropical Itch. This drink was created by bartender Harry Yee, a teetotaler who enjoyed a forty-year career behind the bar.[23] Yee is also credited with creating the Blue Hawaii.

¼ cup plus 2 tablespoons water
¼ cup plus 2 tablespoons passion-fruit juice
1 tablespoon orange curacao or Cointreau
1 tablespoon Kentucky bourbon
   Ice
1 tablespoon Bacardi 151 rum

Mix the water and the passion-fruit juice together. Add the orange curacao and bourbon; mix and pour over ice in a hurricane glass. Float the Bacardi rum on top of the drink.

MINT JULEP

The mint julep, the official drink of the Kentucky Derby, is a simple mixture of bourbon, mint, sugar, a little water, and ice. It can be a very refreshing drink on a warm day at the races. Joe Nickell, the author of *The Kentucky Mint Julep*, offers several suggestions for the perfect mint julep.

- Use only good Kentucky bourbon. As I stated before, bourbon does not need to be made in Kentucky, although most bourbon is made there.
- Use superfine sugar for your mint julep; it will dissolve better than regular granulated sugar. Superfine sugar is also known as baker's sugar, castor (caster) sugar, berry sugar, and bar sugar.
- Serve the julep in a chilled silver julep cup.
- Use crushed ice when making a julep.

- When drinking a julep, don't use a straw (or use a short straw), so that you can savor the aroma of the mint.
- When serving a julep, avoid touching the sides of the silver frosted julep cup so that you won't leave smudges.

Here is Colonel Nickell's personal recipe for the mint julep.[24]

    5 sprigs fresh mint
    1 teaspoon superfine sugar
    2 teaspoons water
      Crushed ice
    ¼ cup Kentucky bourbon

Place four sprigs of the mint, the sugar, and the water in a Boston shaker and lightly bruise the mint with a muddler. This allows the flavor of the mint to seep into the drink. Add the crushed ice and bourbon to a julep cup and stir. Strain the mint-sugar-water mixture into the julep cup and stir. Garnish with the remaining sprig of mint.

STRAWBERRY JULEP

You might also want to try this variation.

    4 strawberries, washed and hulled
    1 teaspoon sugar
    1 teaspoon water
    ¼ cup Kentucky bourbon
      Ice
    1 sprig mint

Place the strawberries, sugar, water, and bourbon in a blender with three ice cubes. Blend the ingredients together. Fill a julep glass with ice, and pour the contents of the blender into the julep glass. Garnish with the sprig of mint.

EGGNOG FOR ONE

Craig Claiborne, the iconic food writer and former food editor of the *New York Times*, wrote *Craig Claiborne's Southern Cooking*, where he lists four recipes for eggnog (three with bourbon and one virgin-style eggnog for children), including "eggnog for one." Having spent his childhood in Mississippi, he advises that bourbon is the proper whiskey to use in eggnog because, for "a dedicated Southerner, no other whiskey, or anything as alien as rum or Cognac, would do."[25] Today one should use caution when making this recipe because of the uncooked egg. It is a good idea to use the pasteurized egg product instead.

 1 egg (or ¼ cup pasteurized eggs)
 3 tablespoons Kentucky bourbon
 1 teaspoon sugar
 ½ cup milk
    Ice
    Nutmeg

Combine the egg, bourbon, sugar, and milk in a Boston shaker filled with ice. Shake and strain into a tall glass. Sprinkle with nutmeg.

KENTUCKY BOURBON SOUR

Some of the drinks featured in this chapter are sweet. That is, you can taste the sugar in the drink. Arguably, humans can taste only six real flavors: sweet, sour, bitter, salt, umami, and hot (or spicy). The details of flavors are in the olfactory sense, or the nose. Generally speaking, mixology is a celebration of the first three, as most mixed drinks are a delicate balance of sweet, sour, and bitter. The other three come into play only rarely in mixed beverages. This next drink is for people who like the sour in their drinks.

    Juice of half a lemon (2 tablespoons)
 1 teaspoon simple syrup
 ¼ cup Kentucky bourbon
    Ice
    Orange slice

Place the lemon juice, simple syrup, and bourbon in a Boston shaker with ice. Shake well and strain the drink into a whiskey sour glass. Garnish with the orange slice.

KENTUCKY COLONEL

The Kentucky Colonel commission is an honorary distinction given by the governor of Kentucky.[26] Once someone is granted a commission as a Colonel, the person is eligible for membership in the Honorable Order of Kentucky Colonels, which exists to "aide and promote the Commonwealth and its citizens."[27] Every year the order provides financial support to Kentucky charitable and educational institutions and organizations. This drink carries the name of these honorable men and women and is an easy cocktail to fix.

- ¼ cup Kentucky bourbon
- 1 tablespoon Benedictine liqueur
-   Ice
- 1 twist of lemon

Place the bourbon and Benedictine liqueur in a Boston shaker with ice and shake until the mixture is cold. Strain into a cocktail glass. Garnish with the twist of lemon.

BOURBON MILK PUNCH

In the introduction I refer to a meal I ate at Dickie Brennan's Bourbon House in New Orleans, a restaurant famous for its seafood and for its bourbon milk punch. This is the bourbon milk punch recipe used there.

YIELD: 1½ QUARTS

- 4 cups milk
- 1 cup Kentucky bourbon
- ¼ cup vanilla extract
- ¼ cup simple syrup
- 1 pint vanilla ice cream
-   Ground nutmeg

Combine the milk, bourbon, vanilla, simple syrup, and ice cream in a blender and blend for 8 seconds. Pour into cups. Garnish with the nutmeg.

ROCK STAR

The Brennan family of New Orleans owns many restaurants, including Café Adelaide, which features a bar called the Swizzle Stick. When patrons order the Rock Star drink, they also receive sunglasses and a rock star scarf. This drink is featured in the book *In the Land of Cocktails: Recipes and Adventures from the Cocktail Chicks*, by Ti Adelaide Martin and Lally Brennan, who are the proprietors of Commander's Palace, a restaurant built in the garden district in New Orleans in 1880.[28] Commander's Palace now has a location in Destin, Florida.

¼ cup Kentucky bourbon (the original recipe calls for Maker's Mark)
¼ cup citrus-flavored energy drink, such as SoBe
1 splash cola

Combine the bourbon, energy drink, and cola in an Old Fashioned glass, stir, and add ice.

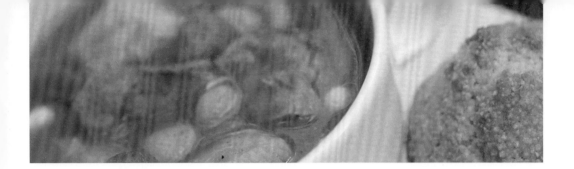

CHAPTER TWO
WINTER

For bourbon distilleries, winter is an important time of the year. As the weather cools, the temperature drops in the storage warehouses, allowing the bourbon to contract in the barrels. During the warm weather, the bourbon has expanded and pushed its way into the burned wood of the barrel. So now in cold weather, the bourbon contracts and pulls with it, from the barrel, color and flavor that will stay with the bourbon until it is consumed. For the bourbon drinker in winter, this whiskey provides relief from the cold by dropping the body's temperature, a phenomenon perceived by humans as a warming sensation.

KENTUCKY BOURBON PANCAKES

One of the great memories of winter is body-warming hot food, such as pancakes fresh off the griddle on a winter morning. The following pancakes were created by Chef Tony Efstratiadis as a dessert, but try them for breakfast too. They were featured in Nancy Miller's *Secrets of Louisville Chefs Cookbook*, volume 2.[1]

4 SERVINGS

6	cups all-purpose flour
1	cup sugar
½	cup baking powder
½	teaspoon salt
1½	cups Kentucky bourbon
8	eggs
4	cups buttermilk
2	tablespoons vanilla extract

1 Stir the flour, sugar, baking powder, and salt into a mixing bowl. In a separate bowl, whisk together the bourbon, eggs, buttermilk, and vanilla. Add the dry mixture to the wet mixture and whisk together until the ingredients are just mixed. Let the batter rest for 10 to 15 minutes. In the meantime, coat a griddle with nonstick spray and heat it to 400 degrees, or apply melted butter after it is hot.

2 Pour about ⅓ cup batter for each pancake onto the griddle and cook until bubbles appear, about 5 minutes. Flip the pancake and cook it on the other side until golden brown. Serve with maple syrup or Blueberry Kentucky Bourbon Pancake Syrup (see the next recipe).

BLUEBERRY KENTUCKY BOURBON PANCAKE SYRUP

What are pancakes without syrup? Here is a syrup recipe I found in the book *Gourmet Cooking with Old Crow*, by Emanuel Greenberg.[2] The recipe originally called for Old Crow bourbon, the bourbon of choice of Ulysses S. Grant, Union general and president of the United States; U.S. senator Henry Clay of Kentucky; and writers Mark Twain and Hunter S. Thompson.

YIELD: 3 CUPS

- 1 cup pancake syrup
- 3 tablespoons butter
- ¼ teaspoon ground cinnamon
- ½ cup Kentucky bourbon
- 2 cups blueberries

Place the syrup, butter, and cinnamon in a saucepan and bring to a simmer. Add the bourbon and simmer for 30 seconds. Add the blueberries and simmer for 1 minute longer. Allow the syrup to cool a bit before serving.

KENTUCKY BOURBON FRENCH TOAST

Another breakfast food that goes well with syrup is called *pain perdu* (lost bread) in France, "Poor knights of Windsor" in Great Britain, and French toast in the United States. In my first sous-chef position, where I was in charge of the breakfast menu, our French toast was "Brioche French Toast." Brioche is an egg-and-butter bread; it was dipped in an egg-cream mixture and then fried in clarified butter. Most diners could not finish the dish because it was so rich. Here is my version of French toast.

4 SERVINGS

  2 cups whole milk
⅓ cup Kentucky bourbon
  5 eggs
½ cup sugar
  2 teaspoons ground cinnamon
12 slices egg bread

Mix the milk, eggs, sugar, bourbon, and cinnamon together. Melt butter on a hot griddle. Dip the bread in the batter. Place the battered bread on the griddle and cook until the first side begins to turn golden brown. Flip the French toast and continue to cook until the other side is golden brown too. Serve with butter, berries, and/or syrup.

HOT BUTTERED KENTUCKY BOURBON OATMEAL

Another classic breakfast for cold mornings is oatmeal. Although oatmeal is noted as a cholesterol-lowering food, the butter and cream in this recipe negate any gains you might see by eating the oatmeal. Instead of cream and butter, you can substitute skim milk if you are on a heart-healthy diet.

1 SERVING

- 1 bowl hot cooked oatmeal
- 1 tablespoon butter
- 1 tablespoon brown sugar
- 1 tablespoon Kentucky bourbon
  Cream
  Salt

NOTE:
This recipe will work best if the oatmeal has been cooked a little longer than usual to develop a nutty, thick oatmeal.

Stir into the oatmeal the butter, brown sugar, and bourbon. Add the cream, salt, and more brown sugar to taste.

BLACK BEAN AND KENTUCKY BOURBON SOUP

This recipe for black bean and bourbon soup comes from Panache, a French restaurant in Indianapolis. According to Joan S. Todd's *Taste of Indianapolis: Recipes from the City's Best Restaurant Kitchens*, published in 1996, the chef-owner of Panache was Richard Cottance and this black bean and bourbon soup was one of the featured items on his menu.[3]

4 SERVINGS

Soup

- ¾ cup finely diced onions
- ½ cup finely diced carrots
- ½ cup finely diced celery
- 1 tablespoon minced fresh garlic
- 1 teaspoon ground cumin
- 1 tablespoon finely minced fresh oregano
- 1 pinch ground cayenne pepper
- 1 cup plus ½ cup cooked black beans
- 3 cups rich chicken stock
- Salt and black pepper

Garnishes

- 4 tablespoons Kentucky bourbon
- 4 tablespoons sour cream
- Diced tomatoes
- Fresh cilantro sprigs

1 Sweat the onions, carrots, and celery in a large saucepan, covered, over very low heat until the vegetables are tender but not browned. Add the garlic, cumin, oregano, and cayenne. Cook 4 to 5 minutes. Add the 1 cup of black beans and the chicken stock, and bring the combination to a boil; reduce heat and simmer for 10 minutes.

2 Puree the combination in a food processor until fairly smooth, and then return it to the pan. Add the ½ cup of reserved beans and heat to a simmer. Season with salt and black pepper to taste. Serve in heated bowls, adding to each bowl 1 tablespoon bourbon, 1 tablespoon sour cream, diced tomatoes, and a sprig of fresh cilantro.

PORK TENDERLOIN IN SPICED APPLE KENTUCKY BOURBON SAUCE

Pork and apple are a classic combination that every chef learns early in his or her career. Here the apple is in the form of juice, flavored and thickened to form a sauce for the pork. This recipe, which comes from *A Love Affair with Southern Cooking*, by Jean Anderson,[4] could easily be served with sweet potatoes (also traditionally combined with pork and bourbon) or with a rice pilaf.

6 SERVINGS

3	pounds boned rolled pork loin
½	teaspoon freshly ground pepper
2	tablespoons spicy brown mustard
1	cup apple juice
¼	cup Kentucky bourbon
1¼	cups plus ½ cup chicken broth
½	cup half-and-half
5	tablespoons all-purpose flour
½	teaspoon salt

1 Rub the pork with the pepper and place in a medium roasting pan. Mix the mustard, apple juice, and bourbon until smooth. Brush the pork with the mixture and let stand for 30 minutes at room temperature. While it rests, preheat the oven to 425 degrees. Baste the pork with the bourbon mixture again, and place the pork in the preheated oven for 45 minutes or until the pork reaches an internal temperature of 150 degrees.

2 To make the sauce: Deglaze the roasting pan with the remaining bourbon mixture; then pour the deglazing mixture into a saucepan and boil for 2 minutes. Stir in the 1¼ cups chicken broth and the half-and-half. Mix the ½ cup broth with the flour and salt, add the flour mixture to the saucepan, and mix. Cook over medium heat until the mixture thickens.

3 Slice the pork and serve with mashed potatoes and the apple-bourbon sauce.

CHICKEN KENTUCKIANA

This recipe is named for Metro Louisville and its surroundings, including an area across the Ohio River in Indiana. Indiana is one of the states besides Kentucky where bourbon was traditionally produced. The recipe, which comes from Nancy Miller's book *Secrets of Louisville Chefs*,[5] makes a dish that is wonderful with rice or mashed potatoes.

6 SERVINGS

- 6 (¼-pound) boneless chicken breasts with skin
- ¼ cup flour
- 2 tablespoons oil
- 1 tablespoon butter
- 2 tablespoons minced shallots
- 1 cup sliced button mushrooms
- ¼ cup Kentucky bourbon
- 2 cups heavy cream
- 1 cup baby spinach
- 1 tablespoon chopped thyme
- ½ teaspoon freshly ground pepper
  Salt

1 Coat the chicken breasts with the flour and set aside while you heat the oil in a pan over medium-high heat. Sauté the chicken in the oil for about 3 to 4 minutes on each side; the crust should be golden brown. Set the chicken aside.

2 Heat the butter in the same pan. Sauté the shallots for 1 minute; then add the mushrooms and sauté for 1 additional minute. Remove the pan from the stove and carefully add the bourbon. Return the pan to the heat (don't be surprised if the bourbon flames). Add the cream, spinach, thyme, and pepper and mix well. Simmer the mixture for 2 minutes. Add the browned chicken breasts to the bourbon-cream sauce, bring to a high simmer, and cook for an additional 5 minutes. Season with salt and serve over rice or with mashed potatoes.

CHICKEN WITH MUSTARD HONEY KENTUCKY BOURBON SAUCE

This is a simple dish to prepare and can be served with corn, pasta, rice, or potatoes and any other vegetable that you might have available.

6 SERVINGS

6 (1/4-pound) boneless chicken breasts with skin
Salt and pepper
½ cup honey
3 tablespoons dry mustard
¼ cup Kentucky bourbon
1 tablespoon brown mustard seeds

1 Preheat the oven to 350 degrees. Salt and pepper the chicken to taste and bake the chicken until the juices run clear.

2 To make the sauce: Mix the honey, mustard, bourbon, and mustard seeds. Serve the chicken over rice with the sauce on top.

KENTUCKY BOURBON ACORN SQUASH

A great side dish with Chicken with Mustard Honey Kentucky Bourbon Sauce is acorn squash. This squash recipe can be baked alongside the chicken in the same oven.

SERVES 6

 3 acorn squashes, cut in half
    Salt
 6 tablespoons Kentucky bourbon
 6 tablespoons brown sugar
 3 tablespoons butter
1½ teaspoon cinnamon

1 Preheat the oven to 350 degrees. Remove the seeds from the squash halves and discard the seeds. Sprinkle the squashes with salt to taste. Place in each cavity ½ tablespoon of the butter and 1 tablespoon of the brown sugar. Bake the halves for 30 minutes.

2 Remove the squashes from the oven; place 1 tablespoon of bourbon in each half and dust with the cinnamon. Cover with foil and return to oven for another 30 minutes.

ASIAN KENTUCKY BOURBON—MARINATED CHICKEN

Asian cuisine is one of the places where bourbon use is emerging. The next two recipes were created by Chef Tom Smith, a graduate of the Culinary Institute of America who has served both as a private chef and as the executive chef of award-winning restaurants.

4 SERVINGS

Marinade

    1 tablespoon vegetable oil
    1 teaspoon minced fresh ginger
    1 scallion, minced
    1 teaspoon minced garlic
    ¼ cup Kentucky bourbon
    ¼ cup brown sugar
    ¼ cup mushroom soy sauce
    ¼ cup pineapple juice
    1 teaspoon freshly ground pepper

Chicken

    4 (5-ounce) boneless, skinless chicken breasts, cut into strips
    2 egg whites
    2 tablespoons cornstarch
    ¼ cup vegetable oil
    1 teaspoon minced fresh ginger
    1 tablespoon minced garlic
    1 scallion, minced
    2 cups fresh pineapple, 1-inch cubes
       Cornstarch for slurry
    4 cups cooked short-grain rice

1 To make the marinade: Heat the vegetable oil quickly, and cook the ginger, scallion, and garlic in it until aromatic, approximately 10 seconds. Add the bourbon and allow it to flame. Add the brown sugar and cook until the sugar is dissolved. Add the soy sauce, pineapple juice, and pepper; combine; cool.

2 To prepare the chicken: Place the chicken breast strips in a small nonreactive container (glass, ceramic, plastic, or stainless steel). Divide the marinade in half, and pour half over the chicken, reserving the other half; marinate, re-frigerated, for 2 hours. Remove the chicken from the marinade and pat dry.

3 Whip the egg whites and dredge the chicken in them to coat. Sprinkle the 2 tablespoons cornstarch over the chicken and toss to coat. Heat the ¼ cup vegetable oil in a wok or large sauté pan until very hot. Quickly stir-fry the ginger, garlic, and scallions until aromatic. Add the chicken and stir-fry until the chicken turns white and firms. Add the pineapple and heat through. Add the reserved marinade and toss to coat. Make a slurry by adding equal parts cornstarch and water in a small bowl. Once the two are mixed together, add the cornstarch slurry to the pan and cook until the sauce is thickened. Serve over the rice.

ASIAN STRAWBERRY KENTUCKY BOURBON SHRIMP

In this recipe, Smith exploits what seems at first glance like an unlikely flavor combination but creates a culinary delight.

4 SERVINGS

1½ pounds medium shrimp, peeled and deveined
    Salt and pepper
 2 egg whites
 2 tablespoons cornstarch
 ¼ cup vegetable oil
 ¼ cup Kentucky bourbon
 ¾ cup diced strawberries
 ¼ cup peeled and finely diced Granny Smith apple
 ¼ cup peeled and finely diced honeydew melon
 ¼ cup peeled and finely diced cantaloupe
 1 cup mayonnaise
 ½ cup sweetened condensed milk
 4 cups cooked short-grain rice
 4 tablespoons chopped toasted pecans

Season the shrimp with the salt and pepper. Toss the shrimp in the egg whites to coat, and sprinkle with cornstarch to coat. Toast the pecans in a 350-degree oven for 5 minutes. Heat the oil in a wok or large sauté pan until very hot. Add the shrimp and stir-fry until cooked (they will turn pink when done). Add the bourbon and flame. Add the strawberries, apple, honeydew melon, and cantaloupe and heat through. Reduce heat to medium, add the mayonnaise and condensed milk, toss together, and heat through. Adjust seasonings. Serve over the rice and garnish with the chopped pecans.

KENTUCKY BOURBON BEEF TENDERLOIN

Beef tenderloin is very lean and very tender. This recipe combines ingredients to form a sweet and sour sauce for the meat. The addition of a baked sweet potato complements the sweet flavors of the sauce, while a baked white potato helps foil the sweet and sour flavors.

6 SERVINGS

   1 cup Kentucky bourbon
1¼ cup brown sugar
   ⅔ cup soy sauce
   1 cup finely chopped cilantro
   ½ cup lemon juice
   2 tablespoons Worcestershire sauce
   2 cups water
   1 teaspoon dried thyme
   4 pounds beef tenderloin

Combine the bourbon, brown sugar, soy sauce, cilantro, lemon juice, Worcestershire sauce, water, and thyme to make a marinade. Cut the beef tenderloin into two-inch slices and pour the marinade over them. Allow the beef to marinate, refrigerated, for at least 2 hours (for best results, marinate for up to 6 hours). Turn it at least every hour to allow equal marinating for each piece. Preheat the oven to 350 degrees and cook the tenderloin in the oven until done (the meat should be pink inside), about 20 minutes. Cut into serving-size pieces.

WINDSOR MINCEMEAT

This is an adaptation of a recipe used by Swiss chef Gabriel Tschumi for the British royal family in the early twentieth century. It is taken from his book *Royal Chef: Recollections of Life in Royal Households from Queen Victoria to Queen Mary*. Because the original Windsor mincemeat recipe was a huge undertaking yielding 675 pounds of mincemeat, I scaled it back considerably. I also replaced brandy with bourbon and made a few other ingredient substitutions. Tschumi wrote that this mincemeat was served at Windsor Castle each Christmas during Queen Victoria's reign.

In the *Old Bardstown Bourbon Cookbook*, published by the Willett Distilling Company in 1967, you may find recipes for mincemeat cake, mincemeat pumpkin pie, and mincemeat cookies, in addition to mincemeat pie.

YIELD: 8 POUNDS OR 16 CUPS

- 1 pound currants
- 1 cup orange peel
- 1 cup lemon peel
- 1 cup citron
- 2 tablespoons cinnamon
- 2 tablespoons allspice
- 2 tablespoons ground cloves
- 2 tablespoons nutmeg
- 2 tablespoons white sugar
- 1 cup turbinado sugar
- 1¼ pounds ground beef
- 1¼ pounds beef suet
- 2½ quarts peeled, cored, and sliced Granny Smith apples
- 1 tablespoon lemon juice
- ¾ cup Kentucky bourbon
- 1 double piecrust (see Kentucky Bourbon Pastry, page 31)

NOTE:
Leftover mincemeat may be frozen in three-cup units for later use.

Pass the currants, orange peel, lemon peel, citron, cinnamon, allspice, cloves, nutmeg, white sugar, turbinado sugar, ground beef, beef suet, and apples through a coarse sausage grinder. Mix in a very large bowl. After mixing, stir in the lemon juice and bourbon. Preheat the oven to 425 degrees. For each pie, place 3 cups of mincemeat in a 9-inch piecrust, top with another piecrust, and bake until the top crust is golden brown.

KENTUCKY BOURBON PASTRY

Pie pastry can be made before or after the filling is made. When the dough is made before the filling, it can be stored as a ball in the refrigerator. Here is a simple recipe for pie dough that can be used with the mincemeat pie.

2 PIECRUSTS

- 2 cups flour
- ½ teaspoon salt
- 6 ounces (1½ sticks) butter or ¾ cup lard
  3 to 5 teaspoons cold Kentucky bourbon

Sift the flour and salt together. Cut the butter into cubes and work the cubes of butter into the flour with your fingers or a pastry blender until the flour-butter mixture resembles cornmeal. Add the bourbon gradually, working it into the flour until the dough forms a ball. Do not overwork the dough. Wrap the dough ball in plastic wrap and place in the refrigerator for at least 10 minutes; on a lightly floured surface, roll out piecrusts. Line a 9-inch pie pan with half of the dough. Add Windsor Mincemeat or other filling (about 3 cups of filling). Roll the other half of the dough into a circle to serve as the top crust. Cut vents in the top crust.

BUCKINGHAM PALACE PLUM PUDDING

Chef Tschumi reports that plum pudding was another Windsor tradition, served every year during his tenure there. Pudding was banned by the Puritans in England from 1664 to 1714, but King George I reintroduced it to the British Christmas table. By the Victorian era, pudding had become a well-established tradition, and Queen Elizabeth II still gives each staff person a plum pudding for Christmas. Americans may not realize that a British pudding is more like a cake than like a Jell-O pudding. Also, the *plum* in *plum pudding* refers to raisins. This recipe, like the mincemeat recipe, has been scaled way down from the original Tschumi recipe.

YIELD: 5 (2-POUND) PUDDINGS

 2 pounds flour
 1 pound turbinado sugar
 1⅓ pounds currants
 1⅓ pounds raisins
 1 pound candied citrus peel
 1⅔ pounds beef suet
 ¼ cup allspice
 2 cups beer
 5 eggs, beaten
 ⅓ cup plus 2 tablespoons Kentucky bourbon

1 Mix together the flour, sugar, currants, raisins, citrus peel, beef suet, and allspice in a very large bowl. Stir in the beaten eggs, then the beer, then the bourbon.

2 Divide the pudding into five equal portions of approximately 2 pounds each. Wrap each portion in a piece of cheesecloth dusted with flour and tie at the top with string, leaving string ends of at least 8 inches. Bring water to a simmer in a pot with handles. Tie the string ends of the wrapped pudding to the pot handles so that the pudding is suspended in the water and does not touch the bottom of the pot. Simmer uncovered for 8 hours, adding additional water to the pot as needed to cover the pudding.

KENTUCKY COLONEL BOURBON BALLS

Bourbon balls are a classic winter confection. In *The Art of Southern Cooking*, Mildred Evans Warren creates a bourbon ball that does not utilize old cake as some recipes do.[6] Instead she combines pecans, butter, and confectioners' sugar with bourbon and covers the sweet treat with chocolate. She names it after the Kentucky Colonels.

8 SERVINGS

1 cup pecan halves plus additional for garnish
¼ cup Kentucky bourbon
1 pound confectioners' sugar
½ cup butter
1 teaspoon vanilla extract
4 ounces (4 squares) bittersweet chocolate
1 tablespoon melted paraffin

1 Soak the 1 cup of pecans in bourbon for several hours. Mix the sugar, butter, and vanilla until creamy. Drain the pecans, reserving the bourbon liquid that remains; mix the liquid into the sugar mixture.

2 Roll the sugar mixture into marble-sized balls around the pecan halves. Chill the balls in the refrigerator for 1 hour.

3 Melt the chocolate and add the paraffin. Dip the cooled balls into the melted chocolate; use a fork to retrieve the balls from the melted chocolate mixture. Top each ball with a pecan half and allow to dry.

KENTUCKY BOURBON BALLS

These bourbon balls contain graham cracker crumbs. Graham crackers were developed in 1829 by a Presbyterian minister, the Reverend Sylvester Graham, who was a vegetarian teetotaler and preached that a bland diet of mostly fruits, vegetables, and high-fiber grains would help people avoid "impure thoughts." If he were alive today, Graham would be proud to know that he has been very influential in the vegan movement and lifestyle; however he would be horrified to learn that rich confections such as piecrust, s'mores, and these bourbon balls are created utilizing the cracker named for him.

YIELD: ABOUT 48 BALLS

- 1 cup fine graham crackers crumbs
- 1 cup confectioners' sugar, sifted
- ½ teaspoon vanilla extract
- 1 cup chopped pecans
- 2 tablespoons cocoa
- 2 tablespoons honey
- ¼ cup Kentucky bourbon
- 1 cup superfine sugar

Combine the graham cracker crumbs, confectioners' sugar, vanilla, pecans, and cocoa and mix well. Add the honey and bourbon and mix well. Shape into ¾-inch balls and coat in the superfine sugar. Store in an airtight container until ready to serve.

KENTUCKY BOURBON BREAD PUDDING WITH KENTUCKY BOURBON SAUCE 1

One of the great uses for stale French bread is bread pudding. This recipe is based on one featured in Nancy Miller's book *Secrets of Louisville Chefs*.[7] Both the pudding and the sauce should be served warm.

12 SERVINGS

Pudding

- ½ cup raisins
- ½ cup Kentucky bourbon
- 2 cups sugar
- 2 cups warm water
- 1½ cups half-and-half
- 6 tablespoons unsalted butter, melted
- 1 pinch nutmeg
- 5 eggs, lightly beaten
- 1 (12-ounce) loaf stale French bread, cut into small pieces

Sauce

- 1 cup honey
- 2 tablespoons unsalted butter
- ¼ cup Kentucky bourbon
- ½ teaspoon vanilla extract

1   *To make the pudding*: Soak the raisins in the ½ cup bourbon in a small bowl for 1 hour. In a large bowl, dissolve the sugar in the warm water. Drain the raisins, reserving the bourbon for use in the sauce. Stir together the half-and-half, melted butter, raisins, nutmeg, and eggs. Stir the bread in. Let this mixture sit for 45 minutes. Preheat the oven to 375 degrees and grease a 9 × 13-inch pan. Pour the pudding into the pan and bake about 35 minutes or until golden brown. Serve with the bourbon sauce.

2   *To make the sauce*: Combine the honey, butter, bourbon, and vanilla in a small saucepan. Heat until warmed.

KENTUCKY BOURBON SAUCE 2

Here is an alternative bourbon sauce to try with the bread pudding, made from leftovers from the Kentucky Colonel bourbon balls. This sauce adds a chocolate flavor. I found the recipe in *Kentucky's Best: Fifty Years of Great Recipes*, by Linda Allison-Lewis.[8]

4 SERVINGS

16 Kentucky Colonel bourbon balls
¼ cup whole milk

Slowly melt the bourbon balls with the milk in a pot on the stove or in the microwave. Stir the mixture until the bourbon balls and milk melt together. Do not allow the mixture to boil.

KENTUCKY BOURBON FRUITCAKE

A good fruitcake is a part of the southern Christmas ritual. In the nineteenth century and the first half of the twentieth, fruitcakes were prepared early in the year, because it was believed that the cake would improve as it aged and as more bourbon flavor was deposited into it over the months. Some thought the best fruitcakes were those made the previous year and reinforced every four weeks with another shot of bourbon. Today we are more careful about food safety, but still a fruitcake that is kept cool will be safe for up to a year. If you are willing to invest the time and effort needed to make a fruitcake, here is a good recipe.

SERVES 16

2 pounds seedless raisins
1 pound currants
1 pound citron
1 cup whole almonds
1 cup pecan halves
  Juice and grated zest of half an orange
2 tablespoons plus 1 cup butter, softened
4 tablespoons plus 2 cups flour
1½ cup sugar

6 egg yolks, lightly beaten

6 egg whites, beaten until stiff

2 tablespoons cane syrup

1 tablespoon Kentucky bourbon

¼ teaspoon allspice

⅛ teaspoon cinnamon

¼ teaspoon ground cloves

¼ teaspoon ginger

¼ teaspoon nutmeg

1 Chop and mix together the raisins, currants, citron, almonds, pecans, orange juice, and orange zest. Dredge these ingredients with 2 tablespoons of the flour; set aside.

2 Line a ring mold cake pan with wax paper; cut the paper to fit the bottom and use strips to line the sides. Rub the paper with the 2 tablespoons of butter and lightly sprinkle the buttered paper with 2 tablespoons of the flour. Set the pan aside and preheat the oven to 250 degrees.

3 Beat the 1 cup of butter with an electric mixer until creamy. Add the sugar and beat until very light in texture and color. Add the egg yolks and beat until fluffy; then fold in the stiff egg whites. Add the cane syrup. Add the 2 cups of flour little by little to the cake mixture, beating after each addition. Add the bourbon and beat well. Add the allspice, cinnamon, cloves, ginger, and nutmeg; then add the fruit and nut mixture and beat well again. Pour the mixture into the prepared ring mold and cover it with aluminum foil.

4 Place a pan of water in the oven along with the ring mold. Bake the cake for 4 hours or until a toothpick comes out clean. Uncover the cake for the last 30 minutes of baking. Allow the cake to cool completely; then wrap it and store it in a cool place. Every four weeks, pour ¼ cup of bourbon over the cake (the cake will keep for up to a year). Serve the fruitcake in very thin slices.

KENTUCKY BOURBON–PECAN CRÈME BRÛLÉE WITH CHOCOLATE SAUCE

Chef Dean Fearing, who is called the father of southwest cuisine and is known for his long service to the Mansion on Turtle Creek in Dallas, Texas, is a Kentucky native. He honors Kentucky by incorporating in his cookbook *Southwest Cuisine: Blending Asia and the Americas* several recipes from Kentucky cuisine. And he uses bourbon in several of his recipes. This Fearing recipe has been adapted for the home cook.[9]

6 SERVINGS

Crème Brûlée

6	large egg yolks
1¼	cup sugar
3	cups heavy cream
1	teaspoon vanilla extract
¼	cup Kentucky bourbon
1	cup pecan halves

Chocolate Sauce

2	cups semisweet chocolate chips
5	teaspoons heavy cream
1	cup milk
¼	cup sugar
2½	tablespoons unsalted butter

Caramel Glaze

Sugar (about 1 cup)
Dark brown sugar (about 1 cup)

1 *To make the Crème Brûlée*: Combine the egg yolks with the sugar, cream, vanilla, and bourbon in a saucepan. Heat the mixture, stirring constantly, until it is barely warm to the touch. Preheat oven to 350 degrees. Boil water on the stove, and pour the boiling water into a 9 × 13-inch pan to a ½-inch depth. Distribute the pecans among six ramekins or custard bowls, and pour the cream mixture over the pecans. Place the cream-filled ramekins in the pan partially filled with hot water. Bake 30 minutes or until the custard is set. Remove the ramekins from the pan. When they are cool, chill them in the refrigerator.

2 *To make the chocolate sauce*: Place the chocolate chips in a medium bowl. Combine the cream, milk, sugar, and butter in a saucepan over medium heat and bring the mixture to a boil. When it boils, pour it over the chocolate chips and stir until the chocolate is melted and smooth. Keep warm until served.

3 *To make the Caramel Glaze*: Mix the sugar and brown sugar. Remove the ramekins from the refrigerator and top them with equal parts of the sugar mixture. Use a blowtorch to melt the sugars; then drizzle the chocolate sauce on top. *Caution*: the blowtorch will be very hot and can cause severe burns.

CHAPTER THREE

SPRING

S pring in Kentucky signals not only the greening of the countryside but also the return of horse racing and the culmination of the basketball season. The greenery and horse racing are gastronomically joined in the traditional drink of the Kentucky Derby, the mint julep, which combines two local ingredients, mint and bourbon (*see* Mint Julep, page 12). For college basketball fans, spring brings March Madness, or the NCAA Basketball Tournament, during which drinks laced with bourbon, appetizers, and finger food are enjoyed while fans cheer for their favorite teams.

KENTUCKY BOURBON PRAWNS

Although shrimp would not have been served at the inaugural Kentucky Derby, shrimp can now be brought from distant sites to serve. Furthermore, many farmers in Kentucky have turned to producing freshwater prawns. So here we have a combination of bourbon and freshwater prawns that could easily be featured at a modern Derby party and would both be grown in Kentucky.

6 SERVINGS

- 6 tablespoons plus 6 tablespoons cold butter
- 2 cups brown sugar
- ¾ teaspoon minced garlic
- 1½ teaspoons minced shallots
    Juice of 1½ lemons
- ¼ cup and 2 tablespoons white wine
- ¾ cup Worcestershire sauce
- 1½ teaspoons Tabasco
- ¼ cup and 2 tablespoons Kentucky bourbon
- 1½ pounds Kentucky freshwater prawns, peeled and deveined

In a sauté pan melt 6 tablespoons of the butter. Add the brown sugar, garlic, and shallots and cook on high heat until the shallots become translucent. Deglaze the pan with the lemon juice and white wine. Boil until the liquid has been reduced by one-third. Add the Worcestershire sauce, Tabasco, bourbon, and prawns to the pan. Reduce heat to a simmer and turn the prawns to cook them on both sides until pink. Finish the dish with the remaining cold butter.

KENTUCKY BOURBON BLINI WITH CAVIAR

This recipe makes an upscale Derby appetizer. Kentucky spoonfish or paddlefish caviar is recommended. Some of the benefits of spoonfish caviar are that it has a smooth flavor, it costs a fraction of what the top-rated beluga costs, and for Kentuckians this culinary treat is local.

30 SERVINGS

> Kentucky Bourbon Pancakes, page 18
> Sour cream
> Caviar

Follow the Kentucky Bourbon Pancakes recipe, but dip only about 1 tablespoon of batter onto the griddle for each pancake; pancakes of this size are called blini. Top the blini with a little sour cream and place the caviar on the sour cream.

KENTUCKY BOURBON CHICKEN WINGS

Another appetizer that's great for Derby is chicken wings—but then they are the perfect appetizer all year long. This is a simple dish as easy to prepare as it is to eat.

6 SERVINGS

- 24 chicken wings with skin
- ¼ cup Kentucky bourbon
- 2 tablespoons olive oil
- 1 tablespoon finely chopped lemon zest
- 3 tablespoons lemon juice (the juice of 1 lemon)
- 1 cup fine, dry bread crumbs, unseasoned
- 1 tablespoon sweet Hungarian paprika
-    Salt and pepper

1 Cut each wing into three pieces. Discard the wing tips or save them for chicken stock. Combine the wing pieces, bourbon, olive oil, lemon zest, and lemon juice in a bowl. Toss to coat the wings, and marinate them for at least 2 hours in the refrigerator.

2 Preheat the oven to 350 degrees. Mix the bread crumbs and paprika, along with salt and pepper to taste, in a plastic bag. Drain the wings and place them in the bag with the bread crumbs. Shake the bag to coat the wings with the crumb mixture. Place the wings on a baking sheet.

3 Bake until done, about 15 minutes. The wings will be done when the juices that run off are clear.

CANDIED KENTUCKY BOURBON–BACON BITES

This simple recipe is adapted from *Paula Deen's the Deen Family Cookbook*, the most recent book by the "Dean of Southern Cuisine." Deen is a native of Georgia but has a connection to Kentucky through her appearance as Aunt Dora in the Cameron Crowe movie *Elizabethtown*.

20 SERVINGS

- ¾ pound bacon
- 2 tablespoons Kentucky bourbon
- ½ cup packed light brown sugar

1 Preheat the oven to 350 degrees. Select a baking sheet that has a lip, and line it with foil; place a wire rack on the foil. Arrange the bacon strips close together in a single layer on the rack, brush them with the bourbon, and sprinkle the brown sugar over the bacon.

2 Bake the bacon until crisp and dark golden brown, 20 to 25 minutes. Transfer the bacon strips to a wire rack set over another baking sheet with a lip or lay them on a paper towel-lined plate, to cool slightly. Break each strip in half and serve warm or at room temperature.

ANGEL'S SHARE BISCUITS

When bourbon (or any other distilled spirit) comes off the still, it is as clear as water. The color and flavor of bourbon develop as it ages in a burned or toasted oak barrel. During the aging process, some of the bourbon is lost to evaporation, and this evaporated alcohol is called the "Angel's share" by the distilling and wine-making industry. As the biscuit bakes, the alcohol evaporates to the angels, but the bourbon flavor stays behind in the biscuit. In the United States a biscuit is a roll made with chemical leavening such as baking soda or baking powder. An Angel Biscuit is a biscuit made with yeast and/or the chemical leavening. An Angel Biscuit is half biscuit–half roll. These Angel Biscuits made with bourbon can be served with most meals.

YIELD: 2 DOZEN BISCUITS

- ½ cup warm water
- 3 tablespoons honey
- 1 tablespoon yeast
- 5 cups flour
- 1 teaspoon baking soda
- 1 teaspoon baking powder
- 1 teaspoon salt
- ½ cup butter
- ½ cup shortening
- 1½ cup buttermilk
- ¼ cup Kentucky bourbon

1. Preheat the oven to 400 degrees. Mix the warm water and honey together and dissolve the yeast in the water-honey mixture.
2. In a separate bowl, mix the flour, baking soda, baking powder, and salt. Add the butter and shortening and mix with a pastry blender until the mixture resembles fine cornmeal.
3. Mix the buttermilk and bourbon with the yeast mixture; add these ingredients to the flour mixture. Combine lightly until the ingredients are just mixed together.
4. Grease a baking pan and drop mounds of dough onto it. Bake for 10 minutes or until golden brown.

KENTUCKY BOURBON BEIGNETS

When I lived in New Orleans, my parents used to stop at the Café du Monde for beignets as they drove me to school. These fried pillows of dough, great for dessert or for breakfast, are usually topped with powdered sugar and served with very strong coffee. The addition of the bourbon here enhances both the sweetness and the intensity of the flavor, creating the perfect blend of Kentucky and New Orleans.

6 SERVINGS

      3 to 3½ cups all-purpose flour
  2 tablespoons butter
  ¼ cup sugar
  ½ teaspoon salt
  1 tablespoon dry yeast (1 package)
  ¾ cup warm water
  ½ cup evaporated milk
  1 egg, slightly beaten
  1 tablespoon Kentucky bourbon
  3 cups peanut oil
     Confectioners' sugar

1 In a bowl combine 2 cups of the flour with the butter and mix using a pastry blender until completely blended. Add the sugar and salt and blend.

2 Mix the yeast with the warm water until the yeast totally dissolves. Let the yeast mixture stand for 2 minutes, then add it to the flour mixture along with the evaporated milk, egg, and bourbon; mix well. Slowly add flour until a soft dough is formed. Turn the dough out onto a floured surface and work it until it has a satiny texture. Do not overwork the dough. Roll out to a thickness of about ⅛ inch and cut into 2-inch squares.

3 Heat the oil in a skillet to at least 350 degrees. Fry the squares of dough in the hot oil until brown on one side. Flip them over and brown the other side. Place on paper towels to drain excess oil. Dust with confectioner's sugar.

KENTUCKY BOURBON BURGERS

Burgers are best in the late spring or early summer, when the weather is not too cold and not yet too hot. An outdoor grill with charcoal or gas flame is also preferred to a stove and a pan. The smoke of the grill complements and accentuates the bourbon in the burger—remember that the bourbon was aged in a charred barrel.

4 TO 8 SERVINGS

- 2 pounds 80% lean ground chuck
- ½ teaspoon salt
- ½ teaspoon freshly ground pepper
- 2 cloves garlic, minced
- ½ cup Kentucky bourbon
- 1 cup bread crumbs
- 4 to 8 hamburger buns
- 4 to 8 thin onion slices
- Condiments

NOTE:
If you are using coals, be sure to start the grill at least 1 hour before you want to grill the meat.

1 Mix the ground chuck with the salt, pepper, and garlic. Add the bourbon and bread crumbs and mix well. Separate the mixture into 4 to 8 patties and refrigerate.

2 Start the grill, and when it is hot, place the burgers on the grill. When blood begins to appear on the burgers, flip them and grill until done. Generally speaking, burgers should be cooked to medium well, which means there will be a little pink inside the burger.

3 Place the burgers on buns and dress with the onion slices and condiments.

KENTUCKY BOURBON HOT DOGS

When you're cooking hamburgers, you should consider also cooking some hot dogs, one of America's favorite foods. Spring is a good time to begin eating hot dogs if you would like to take part in the Nathan's Famous Fourth of July International Hot Dog Eating Contest, sanctioned by the International Federation of Competitive Eating. In 2009 the U.S. contestant, defending champion Joey Chestnut, won his third title, out-eating his competition and breaking his own world record by downing 68 hot dogs and buns. This recipe has a sauce that might help you consume a few more hot dogs and prepare for the summer contest.

4 TO 8 SERVINGS

  8 hot dogs (a 1-pound package)
  1 cup Kentucky bourbon
 ⅛ teaspoon Tabasco
  1 teaspoon Worcestershire sauce
1½ cups ketchup
 ½ cup brown sugar
     4 to 8 hot dog buns

Boil water in a saucepan or skillet (enough water to cover the hot dogs) and simmer them for a few minutes. In a saucepan mix the bourbon, Worcestershire sauce, Tabasco, ketchup, and brown sugar. Heat the sauce and simmer until it is reduced by half. Dip the hot dogs into the sauce and place on the buns, adding more sauce to taste.

GRILLED SIRLOIN IN KENTUCKY BOURBON MARINADE

This steak dish benefits from a bourbon marinade that helps break down the connective tissue of the meat, making the meat very tender. It is best when served with a baked potato. The recipe comes from *Splendor in the Bluegrass*, a book compiled by the Junior League of Louisville.[1]

6 SERVINGS

     1 cup beef stock
    ⅓ cup Kentucky bourbon
    ⅛ cup soy sauce
     3 garlic cloves, minced
     3 green onions, diced
        Freshly ground pepper
   2½ pounds sirloin steak

Combine the beef stock, bourbon, soy sauce, garlic, green onions, and pepper (to taste) in a bowl. Pour these ingredients over the steak and allow it to marinate for 4 hours in the refrigerator; after 2 hours turn the steak over in the marinade. During the last 2 hours, start your grill, if you are using coal. Lightly oil the grill rack. Drain the marinade off the steak and place the steak on the rack over the hot coals. Grill the steak to the desired doneness.

ABOVE

Chicken Kentuckiana (page 24)

PREVIOUS PAGE

Kentucky Bourbon French Toast (page 20) *with*
Blueberry Kentucky Bourbon Pancake Syrup (page 19)

ABOVE

Kentucky Bourbon Acorn Squash (page 26)
with Kentucky Bourbon Glazed Kentucky
Country Ham Steak (page 50)

ABOVE

Grilled Sirloin in Kentucky Bourbon Marinade (page 48)

LEFT

Asian Kentucky Bourbon–Marinated Chicken (page 27)

ABOVE

Kentucky Bibb Salad with a Sweet Kentucky Bourbon Vinaigrette, Crumbled Goat Cheese, and Toasted Pecans (page 61)

LEFT

Kentucky Bourbon-Q Sauce for Pork Tenderloin (page 72) *over sliced pork on a bun*

ACROSS

Angel's Share Biscuits (page 44) *with Kentucky Bourbon Apple Jelly* (page 92), *Apricot Bourbon Jelly* (page 92), *and Jellied Kentucky Bourbon* (page 93) *in the background*

ABOVE

*Pan-Seared Salmon with Chipotle Honey-Lime
Bourbon Glaze* (page 69)

RIGHT

Grilled Kentucky Bourbon Shrimp Skewers (page 70)

ABOVE

Turkey with Kentucky Bourbon Sauce (page 90)

LEFT

Kentucky Bourbon Burgoo (page 86)

ABOVE

*Applesauce Cake with
Kentucky Bourbon Frosting*
(page 102)

RIGHT

*Kentucky Chocolate Bourbon
Pecan Pie* (page 54) *with Bourbon
Whipped Cream* (page 101)

BOURBON BAKED HAM

Easter dinner traditionally features ham, the back leg of a pig. Kentucky is known for its smoked, aged, and salt-cured ham, which is typically served with red eye gravy, a gravy made from lard and water or coffee (or both). This ham recipe features a brown sugar bourbon glaze that is perfect for an Easter celebration (or a Derby party) that will not be soon forgotten. You can serve the ham with macaroni and cheese or a sweet potato casserole.

16 SERVINGS

Ham

- 8 pounds fully cooked ham, bone removed
- 1 cup brown sugar
- ½ teaspoon ground cloves
- 1 pound crushed pineapple, with juice
- 1 cup bourbon
- ¾ cup orange marmalade

Red Eye Gravy

- 1 small piece ham fat or lard
- 1 cup water or coffee

1 Preheat the oven to 350 degrees. Peel the skin from the ham. Trim the exterior fat to an even thickness of ¼ inch.
2 Combine the brown sugar and cloves and spread this mixture evenly over the top of the ham. Roast the coated ham on a rack for 30 minutes.
3 Combine the pineapple, bourbon, and marmalade in a saucepan over medium heat. Take care not to flame the bourbon. Pour the sauce over the ham and return the ham to the oven. Cook until the ham is hot, basting frequently, approximately 2 hours. Remove the ham from the roasting pan. Keep it warm by covering it with aluminum foil and allow it to rest for 30 minutes before carving.
4 *To make the Red Eye Gravy*: While the ham is resting, heat the ham fat in a skillet. When it is hot, add the water or coffee and swirl around to mix. The gravy should be a reddish-brown color. Slice the ham and pour the gravy over it.

KENTUCKY BOURBON GLAZED KENTUCKY COUNTRY HAM STEAK

Chef Sam Mudd, the source of this recipe, is a specialist in southern cooking. He served as the executive chef of fine dining restaurants, including the Galt House's Flag Ship Restaurant and the Executive West Hotel, before signing on at Sullivan University, where he teaches basic culinary skills.

1 SERVING

- 1 center-cut country ham steak, about ¼ inch thick
- ¼ cup brown sugar
- ¼ cup plus 1 tablespoon Kentucky bourbon

1 Trim the edges of the ham steak so that ⅛ inch fat remains. Panfry the steak in a hot skillet until brown on both sides; remove to a platter, and keep warm by covering it with aluminum foil.

2 Dissolve the sugar in the bourbon. Discard most of the fat in the skillet and then deglaze with the bourbon-sugar mixture. Simmer until the mixture reaches the consistency of maple syrup. Pour it over the steak.

CHEF VIRGINIA WILLIS'S BABY BACK RIBS WITH KENTUCKY BOURBON MUSTARD SAUCE

Virginia Willis, the author of *Bon Appétit, Y'all: Recipes and Stories from Three Generations of Southern Cooking*, has served as executive producer of *Epicurious* on the Discovery Channel and has worked with culinary personalities Martha Stewart and Natalie Dupree. She shares this recipe with us.

6 SERVINGS

- 1 tablespoon canola oil
- 2 Vidalia onions, chopped
- 8 large garlic cloves, chopped
- 2 cups dark brown sugar, firmly packed
- 1½ cups ketchup
- 1½ cups Dijon mustard
- 1 cup water
- ½ cup Worcestershire sauce
- ½ cup apple cider vinegar
- ½ cup apple juice
- 1½ cups Kentucky bourbon
- Kosher salt
- Freshly ground pepper
- 3 racks baby back pork ribs

NOTE: *If you are using coals, be sure to start the grill at least 1 hour before you want to grill the meat.*

1 Heat the oil in a heavy large pot over medium-low heat. Add the onions and cook until translucent, 3 to 5 minutes. Add the garlic and cook until fragrant, 45 to 60 seconds. Add the brown sugar, ketchup, mustard, water, Worcestershire sauce, vinegar, apple juice, and bourbon. Simmer the sauce until thick and reduced, stirring occasionally, about 1 hour. Season to taste with the kosher salt and pepper and set aside.

2 Start the grill at low heat or preheat the oven to 325 degrees. Liberally season both sides of the ribs with salt and pepper, place the ribs on a broiler pan, and put the pan in the oven; or place directly on the grill. Cook until the meat is tender, occasionally turning the ribs with tongs, 45 to 60 minutes.

3 Remove 1 cup of the sauce to a bowl for coating the ribs. Brush the ribs on both sides with this sauce. Grill the ribs over high heat until brown and crisp on the edges, brushing with more sauce from the bowl and turning occasionally, about 10 minutes.

4 Serve the ribs with the remaining warm sauce.

KENTUCKY BOURBON PORK CHOPS

Another portion of the pig that is great for eating (as if there were any bad part of a pig) is the pork loin, from which pork chops are cut. This recipe utilizes several traditional sweetening agents that combine well with bourbon. The dish is best served with rice or whipped sweet potatoes. This is another recipe adapted from *Splendor in the Bluegrass*.[2]

6 SERVINGS

⅓ cup maple syrup
⅓ cup sorghum molasses
¼ cup Kentucky bourbon
3 tablespoons sweet chili sauce
2¼ teaspoons garlic chili paste
2 onions, sliced
6 (14-ounce) center cut pork chops

NOTE:
If you are using coals, be sure to start the grill at least 1 hour before you want to grill the meat.

Mix together the maple syrup, molasses, bourbon, sweet chili sauce, garlic chili paste, and onion slices. Place the pork chops in the marinade. Marinate for at least 8 hours, turning the pork chops at least once. Drain the pork chops. Start the grill and cook them until only a little pink remains on the inside.

BOURBON AND GREEN GARLIC KENTUCKY SHORT RIBS

Tim Tucker is the executive chef at the Salvation Army's Center of Hope in Louisville, which feeds more than four hundred homeless people daily. Earlier, he worked at one of the finest restaurants in the United States, the Mansion on Turtle Creek, under Kentucky native Dean Fearing. At the Center of Hope Tucker has created opportunities for his clients by opening a twelve-week culinary training program. Chef Tucker offers this recipe with the advice, "I like to eat this with rice cakes, slow cooked local mixed greens and Kentucky sweet and sour beets."

4 SERVINGS

1¼ cup soy sauce
1¼ cup teriyaki sauce
1 cup honey
1 cup molasses
1 whole stalk green garlic (or 1 whole clove garlic)
1 onion, quartered
1 green pepper, seeded and quartered
1 (2 × 2-inch) piece fresh ginger, peeled and thinly sliced
1½ cups beer
¾ cup Kentucky bourbon
½ cup fresh Thai basil
¼ cup chili garlic sauce
2 tablespoons malt vinegar
2 pounds Kentucky-raised beef short ribs
Salt and pepper

1 Mix together all ingredients except the ribs and place them in a four-quart slow cooker.
2 Heat a large skillet and add oil. Season the ribs with salt and pepper and sear them until golden brown.
3 Add the ribs to the slow cooker and cook for 5 hours at 200 degrees. When the ribs are done, they will be very tender and break apart very easily.

KENTUCKY CHOCOLATE BOURBON PECAN PIE

This recipe, which is adapted from a recipe by Chef Dean Fearing,[3] Chef Tucker's mentor, is known by many names, including "Twin Spires Pie" and "Thoroughbred Pie." The pie is similar to Derby Pie, whose name is trademarked by the Kern's Kitchen Corporation.

6 SERVINGS

All-Purpose Pastry

1½	cups all purpose flour
½	teaspoon salt
1½	cups sugar
½	cup very cold unsalted butter, cut into pieces
2	extra-large egg yolks, lightly beaten
¼	cup ice water

Pie Filling

3	extra-large eggs
1	cup sugar
2	tablespoons butter, melted
1	cup dark corn syrup
1	teaspoon vanilla extract
¼	cup bourbon
½	cup semisweet chocolate chips
1	cup pecan halves

1   *To make the all-purpose pastry*: Combine the flour, salt, and sugar in a mixing bowl. Cut the butter into the flour mixture, using a pastry blender, until the mixture resembles coarse meal. With your hands, gradually add the egg yolks and ice water until a ball of dough is formed (do not overwork the dough). Wrap the dough and chill it for 30 minutes before rolling it out. When the dough is chilled, roll it on a lightly floured surface to a thickness of about ⅛ inch Make a circle 12 inches in diameter. Place the dough in a 10-inch pie pan and preheat the oven to 375 degrees.

2   *To make the pie filling*: In a mixing bowl beat the eggs, sugar, melted butter, corn syrup, vanilla, and bourbon. Strain this mixture into another bowl, using a fine mesh. Sprinkle the chocolate chips on the bottom of the unbaked piecrust, and cover with the pecans. Pour the filling on top of the chocolate and pecans. Bake for 35 to 40 minutes. The pie is done when a knife inserted

2 inches from the side comes out clean. Cool the pie for at least 30 minutes before serving.

KENTUCKY BOURBON CAKE

This cake is adapted from the classic text *Out of Kentucky Kitchens* by Marion Flexner and features bourbon and dried fruit.[4] It is very much like a traditional fruitcake.

16 SERVINGS

- 1 pound pecan halves
- ½ pound raisins
- 1½ cups flour
- 1 teaspoon baking powder
- 2 teaspoons nutmeg
- ½ cup Kentucky bourbon
- ½ cup butter
- 1 cup plus 2 tablespoons sugar
- 3 eggs, separated
  Pecan halves and candied cherries to decorate the top of the cake

1 Chop the pecans and raisins. Sift the flour several times. Mix ½ cup of the flour with the pecans and raisins and set aside. Add the baking powder to the rest of the flour and sift that mixture.

2 Preheat the oven to 325 degrees. In a large bowl, soak the nutmeg in the bourbon for at least 10 minutes.

3 Cream the butter and sugar in an electric mixer. Add the egg yolks one at a time and beat until the butter-sugar mixture is smooth and lemon-colored. Add to the bourbon alternate amounts of the butter-sugar mixture and the flour mixture and mix after each addition. Fold in the raisins and pecans. Beat the egg whites until stiff and fold them in.

4 Butter a 9-inch tube pan and line it with wax paper. Pour the cake batter into the prepared pan and allow the batter to settle for about 10 minutes; in the meantime, decorate the top of the cake with the candied cherries and pecan halves. Bake the cake for 1 hour and 15 minutes. It will be done when a toothpick inserted in the center of it comes out almost clean. Allow the cake to cool for a full 30 minutes before attempting to free it from the pan.

WOODFORD PUDDING

This traditional pudding features blackberry jam and a sauce containing bourbon. *Woodford* refers to Woodford County, Kentucky,[5] not Woodford Reserve, a brand of bourbon made in that county.

6 SERVINGS

Pudding

½	cup butter, softened
1	cup sugar
3	egg yolks
1½	cup blackberry jam
1	cup flour
2	teaspoons baking powder
1	teaspoon cinnamon
½	teaspoon nutmeg
¼	teaspoon ground cloves
1	cup milk
3	egg whites, well beaten

Pudding Sauce

4	tablespoons butter, softened
½	cup sugar
1	egg, well beaten
¼	cup Kentucky bourbon

1   To make the pudding: Butter six 8-ounce pudding molds and preheat the oven to 375 degrees. Using an electric mixer, cream the ½ cup butter and sugar together. Mix in the egg yolks and jam. Sift the flour with the baking powder, cinnamon, nutmeg, and cloves. Add to the flour mixture alternate amounts of the milk and the butter mixture, mixing after each addition. Fold in the egg whites. Pour the pudding into the buttered molds and bake until set, about 30 to 45 minutes.

2   To make the pudding sauce: Cream the butter with the sugar. Add the egg. Heat in a double boiler and stir until the mixture thickens (do not boil). Add the bourbon and mix; serve with the hot pudding.

KENTUCKY BOURBON BROWNIES

Brownies are one of Americans' favorite confections. If you especially like the edges of brownies, you might want to buy an Edge Brownie Pan, which allows each slice of the brownies to develop a slightly crusty edge. The pan, invented by 2002 Sullivan University graduate Emily Griffin, has been featured in many magazines, including *Fine Cooking* and *Good Housekeeping*. These brownies are made with bourbon-flavored pecans.

9 SERVINGS

- ½ cup chopped pecans
- ¾ cup Kentucky bourbon
- ½ cup butter
- ½ cup margarine
- 10 ounces (10 squares) semisweet chocolate
- 1 cup granulated sugar
- ½ cup brown sugar, firmly packed
- ½ teaspoon salt
- 5 eggs
- ¼ cup unsweetened cocoa
- 1½ cups flour

1 Preheat the oven to 350 degrees. Place the pecans and bourbon in a small bowl, so that the pecans will absorb the bourbon. After about 30 minutes, or when the bourbon is reduced by about half, remove the pecans to a small baking sheet and reserve the remaining bourbon. Toast the pecans in the oven for about 5 minutes.

2 Heat the butter, margarine, and chocolate in a double boiler until melted together. Remove the pan containing the butter-chocolate mixture from the hot water and allow the mixture to cool to room temperature. Add the sugar, brown sugar, salt, eggs, and the reserved bourbon. Whisk until the ingredients are well mixed. Add the cocoa and mix until it is totally incorporated. Stir in the flour and the pecans.

3 Apply nonstick spray to an 8 × 8-inch pan and pour in the batter. Bake for about 25 minutes or until a toothpick comes out clean. Cut the brownies when they are cool.

KENTUCKY BOURBON BREAD AND BUTTER PUDDING

Chef Antony Osborne, the creator of this recipe, is the dean of Culinard, the culinary institute of Virginia College, and his pastry has been enjoyed by both the Thai and the British royal families. Osborne offers this classic recipe for bread and butter pudding with some advice: "The key to success with this dish is the slow poaching method [a low moist-heat method of cooking], which provides a light, airy, succulent bread pudding."

12 SERVINGS

- ½ cup raisins
- ¾ cup plus 2 tablespoons Kentucky bourbon
- 1 loaf sliced white bread (crusts trimmed off)
- 1 cup melted butter

Caramel

- ¾ cup sugar
- 2 tablespoons water

Custard

- 1 quart plus ¼ cup milk
- 8 eggs
- 2 tablespoons cinnamon
- 1 teaspoon vanilla extract
- 1 cup sugar

Bourbon Sauce Anglaise

- 1 cup milk
- 1 cup cream
- 5 egg yolks
- ¾ cup sugar
- 1 vanilla pod
  Kentucky bourbon to taste (2–3 tablespoons)

1 Rehydrate the raisins by soaking in the bourbon about 1 hour. Soak the bread in the melted butter.

2 *To make the caramel*: caramelize the sugar (see glossary) and deglaze with the water. Place this on the bottom of a 9 × 12-inch or 9 × 13-inch ovenproof dish. Arrange about one-third of the butter-soaked bread on top of the

caramel. Sprinkle with about one-third of the raisins. Repeat this process two more times.

3 *To prepare the custard*: Mix the milk, eggs, cinnamon, vanilla extract, and sugar together. Pour this mixture over the bread until it becomes absorbed and fills the dish. Cover the dish with plastic wrap and hold in the refrigerator for up to 2 days.

4 When ready to bake, place the dish in a bain-marie (water bath) and bake in a convection oven at 180 degrees (top), 200 degrees (bottom) for 45–60 minutes or in a conventional oven at 250 degrees for 1 hour and 30 minutes. The pudding will be a light golden brown on top. Allow it to cool and invert it onto a warm plate.

5 *To make the Anglaise sauce*: Heat the milk, cream, egg yolks, sugar, vanilla pod, and bourbon in a double boiler slowly until the sauce thickens. Be careful not to curdle the eggs in the sauce. Serve the pudding with the Bourbon Sauce Anglaise.

CHAPTER FOUR

SUMMER

For distillers, summer is the season when whiskey warms in the warehouse, intermingling with the toasted oak of the never-used barrels and absorbing the flavors of vanilla, cloves, coconut, and caramel. The flavors gained in this process make bourbon unique in the whiskey-making world. Summer is also when corn, bourbon's primary ingredient, is grown. A successful year for the crop translates into a bountiful harvest that will become plentiful bourbon; failure means elevated costs in production and a shortage of bourbon. Good corn also makes good bourbon. For the bourbon drinker, a highlight of summer is bourbon served over ice and the food that goes with it.

KENTUCKY BIBB SALAD WITH A SWEET KENTUCKY BOURBON VINAIGRETTE, CRUMBLED GOAT CHEESE, AND TOASTED PECANS

The following salad is a great summer dish because of the cool, seasonal ingredients. The recipe calls for Bibb lettuce, also known as limestone lettuce, which was first cultivated in Kentucky by Jack Bibb in the late 1800s. Bibb lettuce is highly prized by chefs and gourmands. I based this recipe on one I found in the 2003 edition of Nancy Miller's *Secrets of Louisville Chefs*.

4 SERVINGS

Kentucky Bibb Salad

- 1 cup pecan halves
- 3 heads Bibb lettuce, washed and patted dry
- 12 heirloom tomatoes or two large tomatoes
- 12 red grape tomatoes
- ½ pound goat cheese
- 1 red onion, diced

Sweet Kentucky Bourbon Vinaigrette

- ¼ cup cider vinegar
- 2½ tablespoons Kentucky bourbon
- ¼ cup brown mustard
- 2 tablespoons honey
- 2 tablespoons barbecue sauce
- 1½ teaspoons freshly ground pepper
- 1½ teaspoons garlic chili sauce

1 Toast the pecans. Preheat the oven to 350 degrees, spread the pecans on a baking sheet, and toast them for about 5 minutes.
2 *To make the salad*: Break the lettuce apart, cut all the tomatoes in half or in slices, and break or slice the goat cheese.
3 *To make the vinaigrette*: Mix the vinegar, bourbon, mustard, honey, barbecue sauce, pepper, and chili sauce together.
4 Arrange lettuce, tomatoes, onions, pecans, and cheese on four plates, and pour the vinaigrette over the salad.

ROCK SHRIMP JENKINS

Chef Dean Corbett has built a national reputation of excellence over the past two decades with his restaurant Equus in Louisville. He is also the host of *The Secrets of Louisville Chefs Live*, on Louisville cable channel 7. Here is Chef Corbett's recipe for Rock Shrimp Jenkins, one of his best sellers at Equus.

4 SERVINGS

- ½ cup cold butter
- ½ teaspoon minced, blanched garlic
- ½ teaspoon minced shallots
- 1 teaspoon fresh chopped rosemary
- ¼ cup light brown sugar
    Juice of 1 lemon, freshly squeezed
- ¼ cup white wine
- ¼ cup plus 2 tablespoons Worcestershire sauce
- ¼ cup plus 2 tablespoons Kentucky bourbon (Chef Corbett suggests Old Forester)
- 1 pound rock shrimp, peeled and deveined
- ½ cup piccata (lemon) sauce
    Salt and pepper
- ½ teaspoon Tabasco
- 1 teaspoon fresh chopped chives

In a hot sauté pan melt 4 tablespoons of the cold butter while adding the garlic, shallots, rosemary, and brown sugar. Stir together until the garlic and shallots are translucent. Deglaze the pan with the lemon juice and white wine and heat for about 20 seconds. Add the Worcestershire sauce and bourbon (reduce or flame the alcohol). Add the rock shrimp and cook slowly over medium heat, turning the shrimp frequently. Add the piccata sauce; reduce heat and add the remaining cold butter. Season to taste with the Tabasco, salt, and pepper. Add the chives.

SWEET VIDALIA KENTUCKY BOURBON SAUTÉ

At the bourbon pairing meal I refer to in the introduction, one of the new friends I met was Wendy Brannen, who has become executive director of the Vidalia Onion Committee. That committee is the source of this recipe and the next, which combine these sweet onions, grown only in a small section of southeast Georgia, with bourbon.

Here, thick slices of Vidalias are braised in butter and beef broth, and then bourbon is added. This side dish is a favorite in the namesake town of Vidalia, where locals like to serve it with grilled steaks, often adding mushrooms to the mix. It also goes well with prime rib and even pork.

4 SERVINGS

- 2 tablespoons butter
- 2 tablespoons olive oil
- 4 large Vidalia onions, sliced thickly
- 1 teaspoon salt
- ½ teaspoon freshly ground pepper
- ¼ cup beef broth
- ¼ cup Kentucky bourbon

Heat the butter and olive oil. Add the onions and sear on high heat for 2 minutes. Add the salt, pepper, and beef broth. Reduce heat and simmer 10 to 12 minutes. Add the bourbon and cook down for 3 minutes.

DRUNKEN VIDALIAS

Vidalia onions, when available in the spring and summer, are easy to add to the grill and make a hearty, tasty side dish to accompany anything from fish to chicken to beef. Here, the famous southern sweetie gets a little tipsy on the grill with a hearty dose of bourbon.

4 SERVINGS

- 4 large Vidalia onions
  Garlic salt
  Pepper
- 1 cup butter, melted
- ¼ cup Kentucky bourbon
- ¼ cup brown sugar
- 1 tablespoon balsamic vinegar

NOTE:
If you are using coals, be sure to start the grill at least 1 hour before you want to grill the onions.

1 Cut a thin slice off the bottom, or root end, of each Vidalia onion, so that the onions can stand upright. Remove the outer skins and core the onions almost to the base, creating cavities about 2 inches wide. Spray the outside surfaces of the onions with nonstick spray, then (using the garlic salt) salt and pepper the sprayed surfaces. Place each onion on a large piece of aluminum foil, and salt and pepper the cavities as well.

2 Mix the melted butter, bourbon, brown sugar, and balsamic vinegar in a bowl and fill the cavities with the butter mixture. Reserve the remaining butter mixture. Gather the foil around each onion at the top and twist to seal the onion. Cook the wrapped onions over indirect heat on the grill for 1 hour and 30 minutes. To achieve indirect heat, allow the coals to stop burning and just glow. Also, place the onions off to one side of the grill. Remove the onions from the foil, warm up the reserved butter mix, and drizzle it over the Vidalias just before serving.

KENTUCKY TOMATO BOURBON SOUP

This recipe and the next one are summer offerings shared by Chef David Dodd, who from 1968 to 1975 served as the special commitment chef in the kitchens of the British royal family.

4 SERVINGS

- 4 tablespoons butter
- 2 onions, chopped
- 4 pounds Roma tomatoes, peeled, seeded, and chopped
- 4 carrots, chopped
- 1 quart chicken stock
- 4 tablespoons chopped parsley
- 1 tablespoon chopped thyme
  Salt and pepper
- ½ cup Kentucky bourbon
- ½ cup heavy cream
- 4 sprigs thyme, for garnish

Melt the butter in a large saucepan. Add the onions and cook for 5 minutes until soft. Stir in the tomatoes, carrots, chicken stock, parsley, and thyme. Bring to a simmer, cover the pan, and cook for 20 minutes. Puree the soup in a blender until smooth. Return the pureed soup to the pan, season it with salt and pepper, and add the bourbon. Stir in the cream and reheat slowly (do not boil), and garnish with thyme.

SEARED SCALLOPS WITH BOURBON VANILLA BEURRE BLANC

Chef Dodd says that although this dish was designed as an appetizer, it makes an excellent light lunch if served with a crisp Caesar salad.

4 SERVINGS

- 1 ounce flour
- 1 cup finely chopped hazelnuts
- 8 large scallops
- 4 tablespoons plus 2 tablespoons butter
- 1 pound leeks, sliced
- 2 shallots, finely diced
- ½ cup dry white wine
- Half of a vanilla bean
- ¼ cup Kentucky bourbon
- 1½ cups cold butter, diced
- Sea salt
- White pepper

1 In a food processor, mix the flour and hazelnuts together and process to the consistency of fine crumbs. Coat the tops and bottoms of the scallops evenly with this mixture, and refrigerate them.

2 Melt the 4 tablespoons of butter and caramelize the leeks; reserve them in a warm place.

3 Sweat the shallots in the 2 tablespoons of butter. Make sure the shallots take on no color. Add the white wine, vanilla bean, and bourbon. Reduce the mixture by half and complete the sauce by adding 1½ cups cold butter a little at a time, whisking all the time, until the beurre blanc is completed. Salt and pepper the sauce to taste. The beurre blanc is complete when it looks like melted butter that is still whole or not broken.

4 Sear the prepared scallops on both sides to caramelize golden brown. Set the hot leeks in the centers of four warmed plates and place two scallops on each. Spoon the beurre blanc over the scallops and serve immediately.

WILTED SPINACH SALAD

Chef John Castro, who leads Sullivan University's student-run restaurant, Winston's, shares this recipe and the one following, Halibut Wrapped in Country Ham. Castro is a graduate of the Culinary Institute of America, and his recipes have been featured in many magazines.

4 SERVINGS

Hot Sweet and Sour Orange Dressing

- 1 cup sugar
- 3 tablespoons flour
- 1 cup cider vinegar
- 1 cup orange juice
- 3 eggs
- 1 cup chicken broth
- 2 onions, cut in thin julienne strips
- ¼ cup grainy Dijon mustard
- 2 teaspoons freshly ground pepper
- ½ cup Kentucky bourbon
- 12 slices raw bacon, chopped

Salad

- 2 cups corn bread prepared by any recipe, or purchased 1-inch corn bread croutons
- ½ cup pecan halves
- ½ cup cooked, crumbled bacon
- 8 cups spinach
- 1 cup orange slices with the membrane removed

1 *To make the dressing*: Combine the sugar, flour, vinegar, orange juice, eggs, chicken broth, onions, mustard, pepper, and bourbon and whisk together. Cook the bacon in a sauce pot until crisp. Whisk in the vinegar mixture and simmer about 10 minutes or until slightly thickened.

2 *To make the salad*: If you are using corn bread, cut it into one-inch cubes. Bake the cubes or the purchased croutons at 350 degrees for 20 minutes or until toasted crispy. A little seasoned butter will help the corn bread become crispy. The pecan halves may be toasted on a separate pan in the same oven, but for only 5 minutes. Toss the spinach with the dressing. Serve the dressed spinach topped with the orange slices, pecans, bacon, and toasted croutons on four plates.

HALIBUT WRAPPED IN COUNTRY HAM

4 SERVINGS

- 4 shallots, minced
- 2 tablespoons butter
- 1 cup Kentucky bourbon
- 1 quart heavy cream
- Salt and pepper
- 4 cups spinach
- 4 (⅛-inch, thin) slices country ham
- 4 (9-ounce) halibut fillets

1 Sweat the shallots in the butter (cook the shallots without giving them any color). Add the bourbon and flame off the alcohol. Add the cream. Reduce by half. Store until ready to use.

2 Preheat the oven to 350 degrees. Wrap the ham slices around the halibut fillets. Sear the ham-wrapped fillets on each side in a little butter. Place them in the oven until the fish reaches an internal temperature of 160 degrees, about 10 minutes.

3 Warm ½ cup of the bourbon cream sauce. Add the spinach to the cream sauce and toss to coat. Add salt and pepper to taste. Serve the spinach and sauce topped with the halibut.

PAN-SEARED SALMON WITH CHIPOTLE HONEY-LIME BOURBON GLAZE

This recipe comes from Chef Jeremy Ryan, formerly of Kentucky, who has returned to his native Mississippi and works at the MGM Mirage at the Beau Rivage Resort and Casino in Biloxi. He suggests using bourbon in a glaze for pan-seared salmon.

4 SERVINGS

   Salt and pepper
4 salmon fillets
3 tablespoons butter
½ cup honey
⅓ cup Kentucky bourbon
½ teaspoon chipotle chili powder.
1 teaspoon lime juice
   Candied lime zest

1 Salt and pepper the salmon. Melt the butter in a skillet. Place the salmon in the skillet skin-side-up and sear for 1 to 2 minutes. Remove it from the skillet and set aside.

2 *To make the glaze*: Add the honey, bourbon, chili powder, and lime juice to the skillet and whisk these ingredients together; heat them on low heat. Let the glaze thicken slightly; return the salmon to the pan and cook the mixture for 3 to 5 minutes or until the salmon is light pink inside.

3 Drizzle the glaze over the salmon and garnish with the candied lime zest.

GRILLED KENTUCKY BOURBON SHRIMP SKEWERS

As summer heat beckons people from their homes to enjoy the outdoors, they return to the age-old cooking method of the grill. There is something primal about cooking meat or seafood over a fire, which contributes a smoky flavor to the food. In this recipe for shrimp glazed with bourbon, the bourbon enhances both the smoke and the shrimp. It is a great dish to serve with rice or couscous.

6 SERVINGS

    3 tablespoons Kentucky bourbon
    3 tablespoons honey
    1 tablespoon lemon juice
    1 tablespoon soy sauce
    2 tablespoons brown mustard
    3 tablespoons minced onion
    ½ teaspoon ground pepper
    2 pounds shrimp, peeled and deveined

NOTE:
If you are using coals, be sure to start the grill at least 1 hour before you want to grill the shrimp.

1 Soak 6 wooden skewers in water for 1 hour.

2 Combine the bourbon, honey, lemon juice, soy sauce, mustard, onion, and pepper in a bowl and mix. Add the shrimp and toss to cover with the marinade. Allow the shrimp to marinate for 2 hours in the refrigerator. Stir them every 30 minutes.

3 Lightly oil a grill rack and start the grill, preheating to medium heat. Drain the shrimp and thread them onto the wooden skewers. Grill the shrimp until pink.

APRICOT AND KENTUCKY BOURBON GRILLED CHICKEN

Chicken is a blank canvas for culinary artists. In this recipe, Chef Mary G. Trometter, an assistant professor at Pennsylvania College of Technology, adds interest to the chicken by the use of a grill and the addition of dried fruit and bourbon. The recipe is featured in a culinary textbook titled *On Cooking*, by Kentucky native Sarah Labensky, who lives in Columbus, Mississippi, and owns several restaurants there.[1]

Marinade

- ¼ cup Dijon mustard
- ¼ cup dark brown sugar
- 2 tablespoons soy sauce
- 2 tablespoons Kentucky bourbon
- 1 teaspoon Worcestershire sauce

- 4 (¼-pound) boneless, skinless chicken breasts

Basting Sauce

- ¼ cup apricot preserves
- 2 tablespoons white wine vinegar
- 2 teaspoons Worcestershire sauce
- 2 teaspoons Dijon mustard
- 2 teaspoons honey
- ¼ teaspoon red pepper flakes, crushed

  Sliced toasted almonds

NOTE:
If you are using coals, be sure to start the grill at least 1 hour before you want to grill the chicken.

1 To make the marinade: Combine the mustard, brown sugar, soy sauce, bourbon, and Worcestershire sauce and transfer the mixture to a shallow glass pan.

2 Place the chicken in the marinade and turn several times to coat it well. Cover the pan with plastic wrap and refrigerate for 1 to 3 hours.

3 Start the grill. To make the basting sauce: Combine the preserves, vinegar, Worcestershire sauce, mustard, honey, and red pepper flakes in a small saucepan and simmer for 10 minutes to blend the flavors.

4 Remove the chicken from the marinade and place it on the grill. Grill, basting with the basting sauce. Continue to baste frequently and grill until the juices run clear.

5 Garnish with the toasted almonds.

Kentucky is known not only for its bourbon but also for its barbecues. The International Bar-B-Q Festival, held in Owensboro on the second weekend in May each year, draws crowds numbering eighty-five thousand. I based this barbecue recipe on one of Matt and Ted Lee's in their book *The Lee Bros. Southern Cookbook*.[2]

4 SERVINGS

⅓ cup Kentucky bourbon
⅓ cup water
1 tablespoon white wine vinegar
1 tablespoon minced fresh ginger
1 jalapeño pepper, chopped
1 teaspoon minced garlic
1½ pounds pork tenderloin
¼ cup sorghum molasses
¼ cup ketchup
½ teaspoon kosher salt
¼ teaspoon freshly ground pepper
1 teaspoon extra virgin olive oil

NOTE:
If you are using coals, be sure to start the grill at least 1 hour before you want to grill the meat.

1 Combine the bourbon, water, vinegar, ginger, jalapeño, and garlic in a bowl. Add the pork tenderloin and turn it to coat. Marinate the pork at room temperature for 1 hour, turning it every 15 minutes.

2 Preheat the oven to 350 degrees. Remove the pork from the marinade and pour the marinade into a small saucepan. Boil it over high heat until it is reduced by one-third. Add the sorghum and ketchup and cook until thickened or about 20 minutes. Season with the kosher salt and pepper.

3 Brush the pork with the olive oil and sprinkle it with salt and pepper. Grill it over medium heat until the outside of the meat is well marked. Transfer the pork to a pan and place it in the oven at 350 degrees until it reaches an internal temperature of 155 degrees, about 30 minutes. Remove the pork from the oven and allow it to stand at room temperature for 5 minutes. Then slice it against the grain and serve it with the sauce made from the marinade.

KENTUCKY BOURBON BEEF BARBECUE

Here is a beef barbecue dish that includes bourbon. Remember that the key to good barbecue is slow cooking. This recipe is adapted from one I found in *Southern Living 1988 Annual Recipes*.[3]

6 SERVINGS

½ cup plus 2 tablespoons soy sauce
¼ cup brown sugar
¼ cup Kentucky bourbon
1 tablespoon lemon juice
1 teaspoon Worcestershire sauce
½ cup water
1 (2½-pound) sirloin roast

NOTE:
If you are using coals, be sure to start the grill at least 1 hour before you want to grill the meat.

1 Combine the soy sauce, brown sugar, bourbon, lemon juice, Worcestershire sauce, and water and mix well. Place the roast in a dish, pour the marinade over it, and cover the dish with plastic wrap. Place it in the refrigerator for at least 8 hours; turn the roast every 2 hours so that the marinade reaches each side of it.

2 Start the grill. Drain the roast, reserving the marinade. Place the roast on the grill at least 5 inches above medium-hot coals. Cook the meat until it reaches the desired doneness, about 30 minutes, brushing often with the marinade.

KENTUCKY BOURBON BAKED BEANS

What is good barbecue without baked beans?

4 SERVINGS

- 6 strips bacon
- 1 (28-ounce) can pork and beans
- ⅓ cup Kentucky bourbon
- 1 large onion, chopped
- ¼ cup brown sugar
- 1 tablespoon ketchup
- 1 teaspoon brown mustard
- 1 tablespoon lemon juice

Preheat the oven to 350 degrees. Fry the bacon until cooked but not crisp and set it aside. Combine the beans, bourbon, onion, brown sugar, ketchup, mustard, and lemon juice in a large ovenproof pot. Bake for 45 minutes or until warmed through. Top the beans with the bacon.

STEAK WITH BOURBON-GINGER SAUCE

The ginger and the bourbon marinade play a sensory game for people who are lucky enough to taste this dish. I found the recipe in *Around the Southern Table*, by Sarah Belk.[4]

6 SERVINGS

Marinade

- ¼ cup Kentucky bourbon
- 2 tablespoons brown sugar
- ¼ cup vegetable oil
- 3 tablespoons minced fresh ginger
- 3 tablespoons balsamic vinegar
- 2 tablespoons red wine vinegar
- ½ teaspoon whole peppercorns
- ¼ teaspoon salt

- 1 (3-pound) flank steak

Sauce

1 cup beef broth

2 tablespoons red wine vinegar

1 tablespoon Kentucky bourbon

Salt and pepper

NOTE:

If you are using coals, be sure to start the grill at least 1 hour before you want to grill the meat.

1 *To make the marinade*: Combine the bourbon, brown sugar, oil, ginger, vinegars, peppercorns, and salt in a saucepan. Stir over low heat until the sugar dissolves. Cool the mixture to room temperature and pour the marinade over the steak. Cover and marinate for 4 to 6 hours in the refrigerator.

2 Start the grill and lightly oil the rack. Place the steak on the grill and cook to desired doneness (for best results, do not cook beyond medium, as flank steak can become very tough if cooked beyond that point). Medium steak will be pink on the inside, and this doneness should be achieved within 10 minutes on the grill.

3 *To make the sauce*: While the steak is cooking, strain the marinade into a small saucepan. Add the broth and red wine vinegar. Boil until the mixture is reduced to three-fourths cup. Add the bourbon and boil for 30 seconds more. (Be careful when adding the bourbon so that it does not flame.) Season the sauce with the salt and pepper to taste and remove it from the heat.

4 Slice the steak very thinly against the grain and serve it with the sauce.

VEAL CHOPS WITH KENTUCKY BOURBON SAUCE

These chops should be served with mashed potatoes or rice and your favorite vegetable.

4 SERVINGS

Salt and pepper
4 (1-inch-thick) veal loin chops
1 tablespoon vegetable oil
¼ cup minced red onion
1¾ cups veal or chicken stock
½ cup Kentucky bourbon
2 teaspoons minced fresh thyme
¼ teaspoon salt
⅛ teaspoon pepper
3 cups peeled, diced Granny Smith apples
4 tablespoons cold butter

NOTE:
If you are using coals, be sure to start the grill at least 1 hour before you want to grill the meat.

1 Start the grill. Salt and pepper the veal. Place the veal chops on the grill and cook on each side to mark the steak. Take the chops off the grill, set aside, and keep warm in a 250-degree oven.

2 In a sauce pan, heat the oil, add the onions, and cook until they are soft. Add the stock, bourbon, thyme, salt, and pepper, and cook until the mixture is reduced by half. Add the apples and cook until they are soft. Add the butter one tablespoon at a time, whisking it into the sauce.

3 Heat the chops in the oven and cook until about medium doneness, about 20 minutes. Medium-done means pink but not bloody on the inside.

4 To serve, place the chops on mounds of potatoes or rice and top with the sauce.

PORK (OR BEEF) KABOBS WITH MUSTARD-BOURBON GLAZE

This recipe comes from the test kitchen of the Kingsford Products Company,[5] a firm known for its charcoal and lighter fluid and committed to good barbecue.

4 SERVINGS

1 to 1½ pounds boneless pork loin roast or beef roast
Salt and pepper
3 tablespoons Dijon mustard
3 tablespoons Kentucky bourbon
¼ cup soy sauce
¼ cup firmly packed brown sugar
1 tablespoon Worcestershire sauce

NOTE:
If you are using coals, be sure to start the grill at least 1 hour before you want to grill the meat.

1 Cut the meat into one-inch cubes and season it with the salt and pepper. Combine the mustard, bourbon, soy sauce, brown sugar, and Worcestershire sauce in a dish or a plastic bag. Add the meat, turn the bag to coat the meat, and marinate for at least 1½ hours and up to 4 hours.

2 Remove the meat from the marinade and thread it onto skewers. Start the grill and grill the meat for about 8 to 12 minutes, until it is cooked through.

3 Serve over rice and with grilled vegetables.

KENTUCKY BOURBON APPLE PIE

This recipe combines America's native spirit with the all-American dessert.

6 SERVINGS

- ½ cup Kentucky bourbon
- ½ cup raisins
- 10 Granny Smith apples
- ¾ cup sugar
- 2 tablespoons flour
- 1 teaspoon cinnamon
- ¼ teaspoon salt
- ⅛ teaspoon nutmeg
- ½ cup pecan halves, toasted
- 1 double piecrust
- 1 tablespoon superfine sugar

1 Combine the bourbon and raisins; let soak for at least 1 hour. Preheat the oven to 350 degrees.

2 Peel the apples and slice them thinly. Sauté the apple slices in a pan with a little butter until tender. Meanwhile, toast the pecans in the oven for about 5 minutes.

3 Combine the sugar, flour, cinnamon, salt, and nutmeg in a large bowl and mix. Add the apples, raisin mixture, and pecans. Spoon the pie filling into the bottom of a 10-inch piecrust (see Kentucky Chocolate Bourbon Pecan Pie, page 54, which includes a single-piecrust recipe; double all ingredients to make a double piecrust).

4 Cut the top piecrust into strips and arrange the strips over the pie filling in a lattice formation. Sprinkle the pie with the superfine sugar and bake it at 350 degrees until the filling in the center of the pie bubbles, about 1 hour and 15 minutes. Allow the pie to cool for at least 15 minutes before serving.

KENTUCKY BOURBON ICE CREAM

To improve on ice cream for a hot summer day, make it bourbon ice cream. You can personalize this recipe by using your favorite bourbon or by adding chocolate shavings. If you decide to add the chocolate, gently fold it in just before you put the ice cream into the freezer. This recipe is based on one from *Southern Living 1987 Annual Recipes*.[6]

YIELD: 3 QUARTS

  4 eggs
  1 cup sugar
  ¼ cup Kentucky bourbon
  1¾ cups sweetened condensed milk
  6 cups half-and-half

1 Beat the eggs with an electric mixer on medium speed. Gradually add the sugar while continuing to mix. Add the bourbon and condensed milk and mix well. Add the half-and-half and mix well.
2 Pour the mixture into the canister of a one-gallon ice cream maker and freeze according to the manufacturer's directions. Generally the canister will be surrounded by freezing salt water and will continue to be churned while freezing the ice cream inside.
3 Once the ice cream is made, place it in the freezer and let it sit for at least 1 hour before serving it.

KENTUCKY BOURBON BANANA FLAMBÉ

This recipe reminds me of the Bananas Foster I had at Brennan's in the New Orleans French Quarter. Here the bourbon takes the place of the rum used in that classic New Orleans dish.

4 SERVINGS

- 4 tablespoons butter, softened
- 4 bananas, sliced
- ¾ cup brown sugar
- ⅓ teaspoon cinnamon
- 1 tablespoon lemon juice
- 1 cup Kentucky bourbon
- 8 scoops Kentucky Bourbon Ice Cream

1 Heat the butter in a pan over medium-high heat. Add the sliced bananas, brown sugar, cinnamon, and lemon juice and continue to heat until the sugar melts and the mixture thickens into a sauce.

2 Remove the pan from the stove and add the bourbon carefully. Return the pan to the stove (do not be surprised if the mixture flames), and cook until the flames subside or the mixture begins to simmer.

3 Prepare four bowls with two scoops of ice cream each. Spoon the banana mixture over the ice cream.

CHAPTER FIVE

FALL

I n early fall, the corn—so important for bourbon production—is still being harvested. For gridiron fans, fall signals the return of football and of tailgating parties before the games. For bourbon drinkers, fall is a good time to travel the Bourbon Trail to see where their favorite beverage is produced. This is also the season for the Bourbon Festival, a tradition in Bardstown, Kentucky. The festival lasts for a week in late September and offers attendees the chance to enjoy bourbon tastings, music, and food; to see barrel-making, and to watch the World Championship Bourbon Barrel Relay.

KENTUCKY BOURBON CORN CHOWDER

This recipe is good for the cool weather of late fall. I adapted it from a recipe that called for Jack Daniel's Whiskey.[1] Now of course Jack Daniel's Whiskey is not bourbon; it is not even made in Kentucky, but in Tennessee. Bourbon enthusiasts might be interested to know that Tennessee was originally a bourbon-making state and that bourbon is still made in Tennessee. When Prohibition came early to the state, in 1910, the two makers of the state whisk(e)y relocated so they could continue production. Jack Daniel's moved to St. Louis, Missouri, and produced . . . bourbon![2] George Dickel, the other Tennessee whisky maker, moved to Louisville, Kentucky, later to Frankfort, Kentucky, and eventually (in 1958) back to Tennessee. So we could say that this recipe comes from a kissing cousin of bourbon.

Chowder enthusiasts may like to know that it's potatoes that make the chowder. Otherwise this would be bourbon corn soup.

6 SERVINGS

- 3 tablespoons butter
- 1 medium onion, chopped
- 4 cups fresh corn kernels or 2 (10-ounce) packages frozen corn, thawed
- ⅓ cup Kentucky bourbon
- 3 tablespoons all-purpose flour
- 2 cups chicken stock
- 2 cups heavy cream
  Salt
  Cayenne pepper
- 2 potatoes, peeled, cut into cubes, and cooked

Melt the butter in a large sauce pan over medium heat. Add the onion and sauté until translucent. Add the corn and cook until the corn is soft. Pour in the bourbon and carefully flame it. When the flame burns out, add the flour. Slowly stir in the stock, cream, salt, and cayenne pepper. Heat until thickened, and add the potato cubes. Heat through and serve hot.

KENTUCKY BOURBON GLAZED PORK TENDERLOIN

Chef G. Allen Akmon, from whom this recipe comes, has worked as a chef in Europe and has traveled extensively through Asia. He suggests that his Kentucky Bourbon Glazed Pork Tenderloin be served either as an appetizer with your favorite chutney or as an entrée with your favorite starch and vegetable.

4 APPETIZER SERVINGS OR 2 ENTRÉE SERVINGS

- 2 teaspoons vegetable oil
- 1 pound pork tenderloin with the connective tissue removed
  Salt and pepper
- 2 cups Kentucky bourbon
- ½ cup blackberry preserves
- ¼ cup maple syrup
- 1 teaspoon minced fresh ginger
- 2 tablespoons soy sauce
- 4 tablespoons butter

NOTE:
For a smoked version of this dish, simply place the glazed pork in a 140-degree smoker with your choice of wood, preferably bourbon barrel slats, for 20 to 30 minutes before roasting the pork in the oven.

1 Heat the vegetable oil on high in a pan large enough to hold the pork tenderloin. Season the cleaned pork tenderloin lightly with the salt and pepper and sear on all sides until nicely browned; then remove it from the pan and set it aside.

2 To the same pan add the bourbon, scraping gently to remove the caramelized particles left from the pork. Simmer the bourbon, keeping a safe distance away from the pan as the alcohol flames off. After the bourbon has reduced by half, add the blackberry preserves, maple syrup, minced ginger, and soy sauce. Continue simmering until the mixture has the consistency of light syrup. Turn off the heat and whisk in the butter.

3 Preheat the oven to 350 degrees. Roll the pork tenderloin in the syrup, coating it well; then place the meat on a pan with a roasting rack and place it in the oven. Baste the pork with the pan drippings and syrup every 10 minutes; roast it until it reaches an internal temperature of 160 degrees, about 20–30 minutes.

4 Let the pork rest while you bring the syrup mixture to a simmer. Remove the syrup from the heat and baste the pork one more time before serving.

KENTUCKY BOURBON ONION SOUP

Chef Mike Cunha, a Louisville food icon, contributes the recipe for this delicious, easy-to-make classic soup that is a favorite with many restaurant patrons. Cunha has served as a chef at the Seelbach Hotel's Oakroom and at the Limestone Restaurant, where he was also co-owner.

2 SERVINGS

¼ cup vegetable oil
2 cups finely diced yellow onion
1 bay leaf
1 sprig fresh thyme
¼ cup Kentucky bourbon
1 cup chicken stock
1 cup beef stock
  Pepper and salt
4 toasted croutons
2 slices gruyere cheese or Swiss cheese
2 tablespoons parmesan cheese

1 In a medium skillet, heat the oil and sauté the onion with the bay leaf and thyme until the onion turns golden brown. Add the bourbon and continue cooking until the volume is reduced by half. Add the chicken stock and beef stock and allow the mixture to simmer for 5 to 10 minutes. Taste it and adjust the flavor with the pepper and salt. Preheat the oven to broil.

2 Pour the soup into ovenproof dishes. Top the soup with the croutons, gruyere cheese, and parmesan cheese. Place the dishes in an oven set on broil and cook until the cheese melts and turns golden brown.

KENTUCKY BOURBON STEAK AU POIVRE

Another classic dish is steak au poivre (peppered steak). This French dish traditionally includes cognac or some other brandy, red wine, or sherry, but here Chef Cunha gives it a Kentucky twist by using Kentucky bourbon. The dish is traditionally served with mashed potatoes or French fries.

2 SERVINGS

- 2 tablespoons vegetable oil
- 2 tablespoons peppercorns, cracked
- 2 (6-ounce) sirloin or flatiron steaks
- ¼ cup Kentucky bourbon
- ½ cup veal stock
- ¼ cup heavy cream
- Kosher salt
- 1 tablespoon chopped parsley

1 In a medium skillet, heat the oil on high heat. Press the cracked peppercorns into both sides of the steak. Sear each side of the steaks for at least 2 minutes; then remove them from the skillet and set them aside.

2 Turn the heat under the skillet to low and discard any excess oil from the skillet.

3 Take the skillet off the heat and add the bourbon. When the bourbon stops bubbling in the skillet, set the skillet over low heat again and cook until the bourbon is reduced by about 80 percent, or until just a thin layer remains in the skillet.

4 Add the veal stock to the skillet and cook for 3 to 4 minutes. (If you don't have veal stock, use a combination of equal parts chicken stock and beef stock.) Add the cream and cook for an additional 3 to 4 minutes. Season the sauce with salt and add the chopped parsley.

5 Add the steak to the pan just long enough to reheat it.

KENTUCKY BOURBON BURGOO

"If gumbo is the national stew of Cajun country, burgoo is the stew of Kentucky," Ronni Lundy asserts in her book *Shuck Beans, Stack Cakes, and Honest Fried Chicken*. Because the stew is made in many different ways with a variety of ingredients, the "Burgoo Song" by Robert Myles claims, "You can toss in almost anything that ever walked or flew."[3] Many early recipes for burgoo include squirrel in addition to chicken, beef, and pork. In Kentucky, Anderson County, which hosts its Burgoo Festival every September, is known as the burgoo capital of the world. Arenzville, Illinois, makes a similar claim. But the French lay claim to the basic concept of burgoo, and it's conceivable that the word *burgoo* arose somehow from the French *ragout* (pronounced ra-goo), also a term describing a stew.

Burgoo makers agree that

- Burgoo should be made in stages: cook the meat first, and then add the vegetables.
- No less than 4–6 hours should be devoted to making burgoo. Some recipes call for a 24-hour cooking period.
- Burgoo should contain more than one meat.
- Burgoo should be prepared outdoors over an open fire.

12 TO 14 SERVINGS

2	pounds pork shank
2	pounds veal shank
2	pounds beef shank
2	pounds breast of lamb
1	(4-pound) chicken
8	quarts cold water
1½	pounds potatoes
1½	pounds onions
1	bunch carrots, peeled and sliced thickly
2	green peppers, seeded and chopped
2	cups chopped cabbage
1	quart tomato puree
2	cups whole corn, fresh or canned
2	pods red pepper
2	cups diced okra
½	cup chopped parsley

2 cups dry lima beans
1 cup diced celery
¾ cup Kentucky bourbon
Salt and pepper
Tabasco
Steak sauce
Worcestershire sauce

1 Put the pork, veal, beef, lamb, and chicken into a large pot. Add the water and bring it to a boil slowly. Simmer until meat is tender enough to fall off the bones, about 4–6 hours.
2 Lift the meat out of the stock. Cool the meat, remove it from the bones, and chop it. Return the chopped meat to the stock.
3 Pare the potatoes and onions and dice them. Add them, plus the carrots, green peppers, cabbage, tomato puree, corn, red pepper, okra, parsley, lima beans, celery, and bourbon, to the meat and stock. Allow the stew to simmer until very thick, about 6 hours.
4 Season to taste with the salt, pepper, Tabasco, steak sauce, and Worcestershire sauce.

ENGLISH PROFESSOR'S KENTUCKY BOURBON MARINADE

Chef Jonathan Zearfoss, a faculty member at the Culinary Institute of America, contributes this recipe, which originated with the English professor who taught him in a class on William Faulkner at the College of William and Mary. The class opened with a dinner party at the professor's house. As students arrived, they were handed a mint julep, and their dinner featured meat marinated with this recipe. Chef Zearfoss also suggests the addition of Szechuan peppercorns, in Chinese called *huājiāo*, which translates to "flower pepper."

2 SERVINGS

- ¼ cup plus 2 tablespoons Kentucky bourbon
- ¼ cup plus 2 tablespoons pineapple juice
- ¼ cup plus 2 tablespoons soy sauce
- 1 pound sirloin
- 1 teaspoon Szechuan peppercorns (optional)

NOTE:
If you cook with a grill that uses coals, be sure to start the grill at least 1 hour before you want to grill the meat.

1 Mix the bourbon, pineapple juice, and soy sauce together. Place the steak in a glass pan and pour the marinade over the steak. Allow it to marinate for at least 4 hours.

2 Heat oil in a pan or start the grill. Cook the meat in the pan or on the grill over medium heat until desired doneness is reached. Cooking time will vary, but about 5 minutes on each side should achieve medium doneness.

CORN BREAD AND COUNTRY HAM-STUFFED CHICKEN BREAST WITH CHICKEN JUS KENTUCKY BOURBON GLAZE

This recipe, a play on classic southern cuisine flavors, is also donated by Chef Zearfoss. He suggests that the recipe can be adapted to roasting a whole bird by stuffing the cavity of the bird.

4 SERVINGS

- 1 cup finely diced country ham
- 4 boneless chicken breasts, skin remaining
- 2 cups prepared corn-bread stuffing
- 2 cups chicken stock
- ¼ cup Kentucky bourbon

1 Preheat the oven to 350 degrees. Mix the ham with the stuffing.

2 Cut each chicken breast so that it has a pocket, and insert ½ cup of stuffing into the pocket; or place each chicken breast on top of a ½-cup mound of stuffing. Place the chicken and stuffing in a pan or a large casserole and cook it about 15 minutes. It will be done when the juices of the chicken run clear.

3 While the chicken is cooking, make the glaze: Simmer the chicken stock on the stove until it is reduced by half; then add the bourbon and simmer the mixture for an additional 2 minutes.

4 Serve the stuffed chicken topped with the glaze and along with your favorite vegetable.

TURKEY WITH KENTUCKY BOURBON SAUCE

Bourbon whiskey is not the only food named for Bourbon County. One of the options when you purchase a turkey may be the Bourbon Red, a domestic breed of turkey first recognized as a separate breed in 1909 and also known in the past as the Kentucky Red and the Bourbon Butternut. The breed was created in the late 1800s by crossing Buff, White Holland, and Standard Bronze turkeys. Here is a great recipe calling for turkey and bourbon that I found in *A Man, a Can, a Grill: 50 No Sweat Meals You Can Fire Up Fast*, by David Joachim.[4] There it is called "Big Bird with Bourbon Sauce."

8 SERVINGS

- 1 (6-ounce) can frozen orange juice concentrate, thawed
- ¼ cup Kentucky bourbon
- ½ cup water
- ¼ cup virgin olive oil
- ¼ cup fresh rosemary
- 3 cloves garlic
- ½ teaspoon salt
- ½ teaspoon pepper
- 1 whole boneless, skinless turkey breast (about 2 pounds; thaw it if frozen)
- 1 cup whole-berry cranberry sauce (half of a 16-ounce can)

NOTE:
If you are using coals, be sure to start the grill at least 1 hour before you want to grill the turkey.

1 Place the orange juice, bourbon, water, olive oil, rosemary, garlic, salt, and pepper in a food processor and puree until the rosemary and garlic are chopped. Pour the mixture into a container and add the turkey breast. Cover and marinate in the refrigerator at least 1 hour.

2 Start the grill and heat it to medium heat. Place the turkey breast on the grill and cook it for 30 to 40 minutes, basting with some of the leftover marinade several times. Reserve the remaining marinade. When the internal temperature of the turkey reaches 160 degrees, remove it from the grill and allow it to rest on a cutting board for 10 minutes.

3 Meanwhile, boil the reserved marinade with the cranberry sauce in a small pot for 10 minutes so that the sauce thickens a little.

4 Slice the turkey breast and cover it with the sauce before serving.

SWEET POTATOES WITH KENTUCKY BOURBON

This is a great side dish to serve at the Thanksgiving table with the traditional turkey. I found the recipe in *Splendor in the Bluegrass*, a book compiled by the Junior League of Louisville.[5] Kentucky bourbon adds a new dimension to the sweet potatoes and results in a classic pairing.

SERVES 6

- 5 pounds sweet potatoes, unpeeled
- ¼ cup heavy cream
- 1 tablespoon fresh lemon juice
- ½ teaspoon freshly grated lemon zest
  Salt and pepper
- ⅓ cup Kentucky bourbon
- ¼ cup dark brown sugar

1. Preheat the oven to 450 degrees. Pierce the sweet potatoes with a fork and place them in a large roasting pan. Roast them for 1 hour or until tender. Remove them from the oven and allow them to stand for at least 15 to 30 minutes before proceeding.
2. Peel the sweet potatoes and cut them into large chunks. Combine the sweet potatoes with the cream, lemon juice, and lemon zest in a mixing bowl. Add the salt and pepper to taste. Using an electric mixer, mash the sweet potato mixture.
3. Combine the bourbon and brown sugar in a large saucepan and heat to a boil. Stir the sweet potato mixture into the bourbon mixture and cook, stirring occasionally, over low heat until heated through.

KENTUCKY BOURBON APPLE JELLY

After the harvest in the fall come canning and preserving. Follow the next two recipes, from the book *Whiskey in the Kitchen*, by Emanuel and Madeline Greenberg, to make jellies for the coming year.[6]

YIELD: 4 (8-OUNCE) JARS

1 cup Kentucky bourbon
1 cup apple juice
3 cups sugar
¼ cup plus 2 tablespoons liquid fruit pectin

NOTE:
To sterilize the jars and lids, boil them for at least 5 minutes in water.

Combine the bourbon, apple juice, and sugar in a saucepan. Cook over medium heat until the sugar is dissolved. Remove the pan from the heat and stir in the pectin. Cool the mixture and pour it into sterilized jelly jars. Cover and seal the jars with sterilized jar lids.

APRICOT-BOURBON JELLY

This recipe originally called for just "whiskey," but I have adapted it to use Kentucky bourbon.

YIELD: 4 (8-OUNCE) JARS

1½ cups apricot nectar
½ cup Kentucky bourbon
2 tablespoons fresh lemon juice
3½ cups sugar
¼ cup plus 2 tablespoons liquid fruit pectin

Combine the apricot nectar, bourbon, lemon juice, and sugar in the top of a double boiler. Place over rapidly boiling water and cook until the sugar is dissolved, stirring often. Remove from heat by taking the top pan out of the double boiler, and stir in the pectin. Pour the mixture into sterilized jars, seal them with paraffin, and cover them with jar lids. (For sterilizing and sealing instructions, see the preceding recipe.)

JELLIED KENTUCKY BOURBON

I found this recipe in a book titled *Fried Coffee and Jellied Bourbon,* by Willan C. Roux.[7] Roux says the inventor of bourbon jelly was horse-racing columnist Joe Palmer, who created the culinary delight for a trainer who did not like to drink at breakfast on a race day.

YIELD: 2 (8-OUNCE) JARS

- ⅔ cup Kentucky bourbon
- 1 tablespoon plain gelatin
- ⅓ cup sugar
- 1⅓ cup boiling water
- ⅓ cup orange juice

Dissolve the gelatin in the bourbon and pour the mixture into the boiling water. Add the sugar and orange juice. Stir well and pour into two sterilized jelly jars. Keep the jars in the refrigerator.

KENTUCKY BOURBON CORN MUFFINS OR CORN BREAD

Jelly and bread are a natural pair, and there is no bread more American than corn bread. Jeremy Jackson, in *The Cornbread Book*, argues that corn bread should be the official bread of the United States. Even though Jackson's book lacks a bourbon corn bread recipe, I recommend the book as a funny, informative read for anyone interested in corn bread. This recipe is from *The Bourbon Cookbook* by Tom Hoge.[8]

YIELD 8 MUFFINS OR SQUARES OF BREAD.

- ¾ cup flour
- 2 teaspoons baking powder
- 1 teaspoon salt
- 1½ cups yellow cornmeal
- 1 tablespoon grated lemon rind
- ¼ cup light brown sugar
- 2 eggs, beaten
- ½ cup milk
- ¼ cup Kentucky bourbon
- 4 tablespoons butter, melted

1 Sift the flour, baking powder, and salt together. Mix in the cornmeal, lemon rind, and brown sugar. Stir together the eggs, milk, bourbon, and melted butter. Butter and flour muffin pans or a 9-inch square ovenproof dish and preheat the pans or dish in a 425-degree oven for a few minutes.

2 Combine the two mixtures and pour the batter into the preheated muffin pans or dish. Bake for 10 minutes for muffins or 30 minutes for corn bread, or until a toothpick comes out clean when inserted into the middle of the bread.

KENTUCKY BOURBON CHILI

As the weather becomes cool and padded men hit the gridiron for another season of NCAA or NFL football, it is the season for chili, a natural companion of corn bread. Here is a chili recipe from Tom Hoge's *Bourbon Cookbook*.[9]

6 SERVINGS

 4 tablespoons butter
½ cup finely diced green pepper
 1 large onion, finely diced
1½ pounds ground beef
 2 (1-pound) cans kidney beans
 2 (8-ounce) cans tomato sauce
¼ cup ketchup
 2 tablespoons chili powder
 1 ounce unsweetened chocolate, grated
 1 teaspoon salt
⅛ teaspoon pepper
 1 tablespoon sugar
⅔ cup Kentucky bourbon
    Hot cooked spaghetti (optional)

Melt the butter in a large skillet with a cover or in a pot and add the green pepper, onion, and ground beef. Cook the mixture until the meat is lightly browned. Add the undrained kidney beans, tomato sauce, ketchup, chili powder, chocolate, salt, pepper, and sugar. Cover the skillet or pot and cook on low heat for 30 minutes, stirring occasionally. Add the bourbon and allow the chili to simmer for at least 5 more minutes. Serve it in bowls, over spaghetti if you wish.

BARM BRACK

Originating with Chef Anna Sandhu, a world traveler with a long history in the hospitality industry, this recipe for Barm Brack is a play on a traditional Irish bread served at Halloween.

YIELD: 2 ROUNDS OF BREAD

- 1 cup Kentucky bourbon
  Peel of one orange, pith removed
- 2 tablespoons strong brewed tea
- ½ cup golden raisins
- 1 cup regular raisins
- ½ cup mixed dried fruit
- 4 cups white unbleached flour
- ½ teaspoon ground cinnamon
- ¼ teaspoon ground cloves
- ¼ teaspoon nutmeg
- ¼ teaspoon allspice
- 1 pinch salt
- ½ cup cold unsalted butter, cut into ¼-inch pieces
- 1 package active dry yeast (not instant yeast)
- 1 teaspoon plus ¼ cup honey
- 1¼ cups warm scalded milk
- 1 egg, beaten
- ½ cup brown sugar

NOTE:
Leftover bread can be toasted or used for bread pudding if it becomes stale.

1 Combine in a small saucepan the Kentucky bourbon, orange peel, and tea. Bring these to a simmer and add the golden raisins, regular raisins, and dried fruit. Stir quickly, cover immediately, and turn off the heat. Remove from the heat and soak this mixture about 1 hour.

2 Drain these ingredients and reserve the liquid. Keep the reserved liquid at room temperature. It should be barely warm to the touch when you add it to the bread.

3 Spray two 8-inch round pans with nonstick spray, or rub with hydrogenated shortening.

4 Sift the flour, cinnamon, cloves, nutmeg, allspice, and salt into a mixing bowl. Make a center well. With your fingertips, break up the butter by rubbing it and the dry mixture between your fingers; or cut in the butter using a pastry blender. Do this as quickly as possible, because too much activity at this point makes the bread tough. Again make a well in the center of the dry mixture.

5 Add the yeast to the teaspoon of honey and 1 teaspoon of the warm milk in a bowl of about 16-ounce capacity. Pour the rest of the warm milk, the egg, and ¼ cup of the reserved warm bourbon mixture into the yeast mixture. Pour this mixture into the dry ingredients and add the sugar. Beat well with an electric mixer and then knead on a floured surface until the batter is stiff but elastic. Fold in the fruit mixture. Preheat the oven to 350 degrees.

6 Cover the bowl with a damp cloth and set it in a warm place, such as on the stove above a lit oven, until the dough has doubled in size. Punch down the dough and knead again for another 2 or 3 minutes. Divide the dough between the two greased pans. Cover the pans and let the dough rise again until it comes up to the tops of the pans (45 minutes to 1 hour). Bake the bread for 50 minutes total. The glaze should be applied halfway through the baking process.

7 *To make the glaze*: Place 2 tablespoons of the reserved bourbon mixture and the ¼ cup of honey in a small saucepan. Bring this mixture to an easy boil, turn off the heat, and keep the mixture hot by covering the pot and leaving it on the stove. You will glaze the pans of bread with this when the bread has baked about 25 minutes. The glaze gives the bread a lovely dark brown color, and the bourbon adds its fragrance while the bread finishes baking.

8 Remove the bread pans from the oven and with a pastry brush, spread glaze over the top surface of the bread. Return the bread to the oven until the top is nicely browned and the bread sounds hollow when thumped on top. After determining that the bread is done, keep it in the pans for 30 minutes before turning it out. Then allow it to cool slightly before serving it with fresh butter.

KENTUCKY BOURBON FUDGE

Joan and Edward "Jon" Bjornson, who founded the Ultimate Sweet Tooth Fudge Company, shared this fudge recipe. They suggest using Maker's Mark bourbon in the recipe.

YIELD: 3 POUNDS

- 3 cups sugar
- ¾ cup evaporated milk
- ¼ cup Kentucky bourbon
- 6 tablespoons butter
- 1 (12-ounce) package dark chocolate chips
- 1 teaspoon vanilla extract
- 1 7½ ounce container marshmallow creme
- 1 cup chopped nuts (optional)

Butter a 9 × 13-inch pan. Place the sugar, milk, bourbon, and butter in a saucepan and bring the mixture to a boil over medium heat. Cook the mixture to the soft ball stage (236 degrees if using a candy thermometer), stirring constantly. Remove the pan from the heat and add the chocolate chips and vanilla. Stir until the chips are melted. Add the marshmallow crème and, if desired, the nuts. Quickly pour the fudge into the buttered pan. Cut the fudge after it has cooled.

KENTUCKY BOURBON PECAN PUMPKIN PIE

Pumpkin pie, a classic fall dessert, finds its way to the Thanksgiving dinner table more often than not. The bourbon and the pecans in this pie serve to announce its southern origin. This recipe comes from *Southern Living 1987 Annual Recipes*.[10]

6 SERVINGS

Pie

- 3 eggs, slightly beaten
- 16 ounces canned pumpkin
- ¾ cup dark brown sugar
- 1½ cups half-and-half
- 3 tablespoons Kentucky bourbon

1 teaspoon ground cinnamon

½ teaspoon ground ginger

¼ teaspoon salt

1 unbaked 9-inch piecrust (see Sweet Potato Pie, page 100, for a piecrust recipe)

Topping

2 tablespoons butter

¼ cup dark brown sugar

¼ cup Kentucky bourbon

1 cup pecan halves

1. Preheat the oven to 425 degrees.
2. To make the pie: Combine the eggs, pumpkin, brown sugar, half-and-half, bourbon, cinnamon, ginger, and salt, and mix well. Pour the pumpkin mixture into the piecrust and bake for 10 minutes. Reduce the heat to 350 degrees and allow the pie to continue baking for 45 more minutes or until the filling is set in the middle. Remove the pie from the oven and let it cool.
3. To make the topping: Combine the butter and brown sugar in a saucepan; stir and cook over medium heat until the butter melts, the sugar dissolves, and the two ingredients are mixed. Add 2 tablespoons of the bourbon and the pecans, and coat the pecans with the sugar. Spoon the pecan mixture over the pie.
4. Before serving the pie, place the other 2 tablespoons of bourbon in a saucepan and gently heat until the fumes are ready to ignite. Carefully ignite the bourbon with a match and pour it over the pie. When the flames die down, the pie is ready to serve.

SWEET POTATO PIE WITH KENTUCKY BOURBON WHIPPED CREAM

This recipe is adapted from Isaac Hayes's *Cooking with Heart and Soul.* Although Hayes gave up drinking alcohol, he made an exception for a "little bit of bourbon" in the whipped cream for sweet potato pecan pie. Quality bourbon has a rich, mellow, sweet flavor that complements sweet potatoes and pecans.[11]

6 SERVINGS

Piecrust

1⅓ cups all-purpose flour

  1 tablespoon sugar

  ½ teaspoon salt

  6 tablespoons chilled unsalted butter

  2 tablespoons chilled vegetable shortening or lard

  3 tablespoons ice water

Sweet Potato Mixture

1¾ cups cooked sweet potatoes or yams

  ¾ cup sugar

  2 eggs

  ½ cup evaporated milk

  6 tablespoons butter, melted

  2 tablespoons cinnamon

  1 tablespoon vanilla extract

Pecan Mixture

  2 eggs

 ⅓ cup sugar

  ¾ cup honey

  2 tablespoon butter, melted

  1 tablespoon Kentucky bourbon

  1 pinch salt

  1 cup pecan halves and pieces

Bourbon Whipped Cream

    3 cups heavy cream, well chilled
    ½ cup light brown sugar, packed
    ⅓ cup Kentucky bourbon

1 Preheat the oven to 400 degrees.

2 *To make the piecrust*: In a medium bowl combine the flour, sugar, and salt. Add the butter and shortening and cut in with a pastry blender until the mixture looks like small peas. Slowly add the cold water and mix until a dough forms. Shape the dough into a disk and roll out on a lightly floured surface until you have a thin round that will fit in a 9-inch pie pan. Place the piecrust in the pie pan and set it aside.

3 *To make the sweet potato mixture*: Combine the sweet potatoes, sugar, eggs, milk, butter, cinnamon, and vanilla in a medium bowl. Mix well and pour it into the piecrust.

4 *To make the pecan mixture*: In a medium bowl, lightly beat the eggs with the sugar. Add the honey, butter, bourbon, and salt and mix until blended. Stir in the pecans and pour the mixture over the sweet potato layer. Bake the pie for 10 minutes. Lower the temperature of the oven to 325 degrees and bake the pie for 1 additional hour.

5 *To make the whipped cream*: Using an electric mixer, in a large bowl beat the cream and brown sugar until soft peaks form; then add the bourbon and beat until stiff. Refrigerate the whipped cream mixture until ready to serve; then spread it on the pie.

APPLESAUCE CAKE WITH KENTUCKY BOURBON FROSTING

The applesauce in this spice cake makes the cake moist. The palate experiences a "pop" of flavor as the bourbon in the frosting complements the spices in the cake. I found this recipe in *Southern Living 1988 Annual Recipes*.[12]

8 SERVINGS

Cake

         1   cup butter, softened
         1   cup sugar
         2   eggs
         2   cups golden raisins
         1   cup chopped walnuts
       ½   cup plus 2¾ cups all-purpose flour
         1   teaspoon baking soda
         1   pinch salt
         2   teaspoons ground cloves
         2   teaspoons ground nutmeg
         1   teaspoon ground cinnamon
         2   cups applesauce

Frosting

         4   tablespoons plus 2 tablespoons butter, softened
         3   cups confectioners' sugar, sifted
         2   tablespoons Kentucky bourbon
    2½   tablespoons milk

1   *To make the cake*: Cream the butter using an electric mixer and gradually add the sugar, beating until the mixture is light and fluffy. Add the eggs, one at a time, beating well after each addition.

2   Dredge the raisins and the chopped walnuts in the ½ cup of flour and set aside.

3   Combine the 2¾ cups of flour, baking soda, salt, cloves, nutmeg, and cinnamon.

4   Preheat the oven to 350 degrees and grease and flour a 10-inch tube pan. Add the flour mixture and applesauce to the creamed mixture in alternate amounts, beginning and ending with the flour. Mix well. Stir in the raisin-walnuts mixture. Pour the batter into the tube pan and bake for about 1 hour

or until a toothpick inserted into the center of the cake comes out clean. Cool the cake in the pan for about 10 minutes and then remove it to a wire rack. Let the cake cool completely.

5 *To make the frosting*: Cream the butter, gradually adding the sugar, bourbon, and milk, and beat until the mixture reaches spreading consistency. Spread the frosting on the cooled cake.

KENTUCKY BOURBON DOUBLE CHOCOLATE CHEESECAKE

This rich cheesecake offered by Chef Robert W. Beighey is a wonderful ending to a meal.

12 SERVINGS

Cheesecake

  1 cup semisweet chocolate chips
 ⅓ cup heavy cream
 24 ounces cream cheese, softened
  1 cup granulated sugar
  2 tablespoons Kentucky bourbon
 ¼ teaspoon Grand Marnier
  4 eggs
  1 pinch salt

Fudge Brownie Mixture

  2 ounces unsweetened chocolate
 ½ cup butter
  2 eggs
  1 cup granulated sugar
  1 teaspoon Grand Marnier or vanilla extract
 ½ cup flour
 ¼ cup chopped pecans (optional)
  1 pinch salt

Chocolate Ganache

1½ cups milk chocolate chips
⅓ cup heavy whipping cream
2 tablespoons Kentucky bourbon
1 tablespoon light corn syrup

1 Preheat oven to 400 degrees. Apply nonstick spray to a 9-inch springform pan.

2 *To make the cheesecake*: In a double boiler, melt the chocolate chips with the cream; mix until smooth and reserve. Whip the cream cheese, sugar, bourbon, and Grand Marnier in an electric mixer until smooth. Add the eggs and salt and blend well. Add the melted chocolate mixture and blend thoroughly. Pour the cheesecake batter into the springform pan. Bake for 15 minutes; reduce the temperature to 350 degrees and bake an additional 15 minutes.

3 *To make the fudge brownie mixture*: While the cheesecake is baking, melt the chocolate and butter in a double boiler. Stir until smooth. Transfer the mixture to a mixing bowl. Beat in the eggs, sugar, and Grand Marnier, and blend thoroughly. Add the flour, pecans, and salt and blend well.

4 Remove the cheesecake from the oven and carefully spoon on the brownie mixture (start at the edges and work toward the center). Bake at 350 degrees for 35–40 minutes or until a toothpick inserted in the center comes out almost clean. Remove the cheesecake from the oven and cool completely. Then refrigerate until it is completely cold.

5 *To make the chocolate ganache*: While the cheesecake is cooling, combine the chocolate chips and cream in a double boiler and melt them, stirring to mix. Remove the mixture from the heat and let it rest for a couple of minutes to allow for slight cooling. When the mixture is blended, smooth, and slightly cool, add the bourbon and corn syrup, stirring constantly. Then let it stand at room temperature for a couple of minutes.

6 Remove the cheesecake from the refrigerator and place it on a wire rack. Pour the ganache over the cheesecake and allow it to set. Serve it after the ganache dries.

APPENDIX

BACON PASTRAMI—WRAPPED SHRIMP WITH TOASTED ANCHO CHILI STONE GRITS AND CANDIED LEMON

....

Bacon Pastrami-Wrapped Shrimp

Bacon Pastrami Brine

3½	quarts water
1	pint bourbon
1	cup kosher salt
12	cloves garlic
3	tablespoons pickling spice
2	tablespoons coriander seeds
8	bay leaves
1½	cups molasses
1	pork belly

Bacon Pastrami Dry Rub

1	cup coarsely ground pepper
1	cup coarsely ground coriander

Wrapped Shrimp

8	jumbo shrimp, peeled and deveined
	Kosher salt
	Pepper
8	toothpicks
2	teaspoons olive oil

NOTE:
You can buy pork belly at a butcher shop. The strips of bacon pastrami not needed for this recipe may be used as bacon or ham in other dishes.

1 *To make the bacon pastrami brine*: Combine the water, bourbon, salt, garlic, pickling spice, coriander seeds, bay leaves, and molasses in a heavy-bottomed pot and bring to a boil, stirring to dissolve the salt. Remove from heat and let cool. Place the pork belly in the cool liquid and make sure all meat is submerged (weigh it down if necessary). Cover and refrigerate 2–3 days.

2 *To make the bacon pastrami dry rub*: When the pork belly has brined, remove it from the liquid and dry well. Rub all sides with a mixture of the pepper and coriander. Prepare a smoker according to the manufacturer's directions; set it to 130 degrees and smoke the belly for 2 hours or more. (The Bourbon House prefers using pecan wood in the smoker.) Raise the temperature to 220 degrees and smoke until the belly reaches an internal temperature of 170 degrees. Remove it from the smoker and let it rest for 1 hour. Chill it well before slicing it into strips.

3 *To make the wrapped shrimp*: Season the shrimp with salt and pepper, wrap each shrimp with a slice of pastrami bacon, and secure it with a toothpick. Heat the oil in a medium sauté pan and cook the wrapped shrimp until it is cooked through and the pastrami is crisp.

Toasted Ancho Chili Stone Grits

½ cup stone ground grits
   Kosher salt
2 tablespoons butter
2 tablespoons finely diced onion
2 ancho chili peppers, seeded and finely diced
1 cup chicken stock
1 cup milk
1 teaspoon chopped fresh parsley
1 teaspoon finely chopped fresh chives
½ teaspoon finely chopped fresh thyme leaves

1 Preheat the oven to 350 degrees. Place the stone grits on a baking sheet and toast in the oven for 7–8 minutes, until they are lightly toasted and have a slightly nutty aroma. Remove them from the oven and let them cool. Salt them to taste.

2 In a medium, heavy-bottomed sauce pot, melt 1 tablespoon of the butter over low heat. Add the onions and chili peppers and cook several minutes, until the onions are soft. Add the chicken stock and milk and bring to a boil. With a whisk, stir in the grits; stir to eliminate any clumps. Remove the whisk, reduce the heat, and cook 30 to 40 minutes until the grits are tender. (Grits can stick to the bottom of the pot and can scorch, so it's advisable to use a wooden spoon and stir often). Add the parsley, chives, thyme, and the other 1 tablespoon butter. Check the seasoning before serving.

Candied Lemon

      2 cups water
   2½ cups sugar
      1 lemon

Slice the lemon into ⅛-inch slices. Place the slices in a small sauce pot and cover with water. Bring to a simmer and cook 5 minutes. Strain and discard the water. Place the lemon slices back in the sauce pot and again cover with water, bring to a simmer, and cook for 5 more minutes. Strain and discard the water. Place the 2 cups water and 2 cups of the sugar in the sauce pot and bring to a boil, stirring until sugar dissolves. Place the lemon slices into the syrup and reduce the heat to a simmer. Cook 5 minutes, strain, and discard the liquid. Pat the slices dry and toss in remaining sugar. Place in an airtight container and store until ready to use.

To assemble the bacon pastrami–wrapped shrimp with toasted ancho chili stone grits and candied lemon: Place equal amounts of grits on four small plates, top with two shrimp, drizzle with sauce, and garnish with candied lemon.

Bourbon Pepper Jelly

½ cup plus 2 tablespoons light corn syrup
½ cup white vinegar
¼ cup plus 2 tablespoons bourbon
½ teaspoon finely diced jalapeño peppers
⅛ teaspoon chili flakes
⅛ teaspoon crushed coriander seed

Place the corn syrup, vinegar, and bourbon in a small sauce pan and cook until syrupy, about 30 minutes. Add the peppers, chili flakes, and coriander.

BROWN SUGAR-CURED DIVER SCALLOPS WITH CHILI-PECAN DRESSING AND CHICORY VINAIGRETTE

Brown Sugar-Cured Diver Scallops

8 very large sea scallops
¼ cup kosher salt
⅛ cup dark brown sugar
⅛ cup sugar
1½ teaspoons freshly ground pepper
2 tablespoons olive oil

1 Clean the scallops and pat them dry. Mix the salt, brown sugar, sugar, and pepper thoroughly. Rub the scallops evenly with the mixture and place them on a nonreactive baking pan or plate. Cover with a piece of plastic wrap or brown paper bag, weigh them down with another pan or plate, and refrigerate for 1 hour.

2 Brush the extra seasoning from the scallops. Heat the oil in a large sauté pan until hot but not smoking. Place the scallops in the sauté pan; quickly sear one side and turn them over. Continue cooking just long enough to get some nice color on the scallops (about 5–10 minutes), being careful not to burn them. Remove them from the pan and serve immediately.

Chili Pecan Dressing

½ cup pecans
2 Anaheim peppers
4 tablespoons unsalted butter
½ cup finely diced celery
⅓ cup finely diced onion
1 tablespoon minced garlic
4 cups diced French bread
1 cup chicken stock
½ teaspoon kosher salt
1 teaspoon sage
⅛ teaspoon cayenne pepper
⅛ teaspoon black pepper
¼ teaspoon Creole seasoning

1 Preheat the oven to 350 degrees. Toast the pecans for 5 minutes and then chop them. Roast the Anaheim peppers for 20 minutes and then dice them.

2 Preheat a medium sauce pot and melt the butter. Add the celery, onion, and garlic and cook until the vegetables are soft, about 6 minutes. Add the pecans and peppers and cook 2 more minutes, until you can smell the nutty pecans. Add the French bread and chicken stock and stir well to combine. Add the kosher salt, sage, cayenne, pepper, and Creole seasoning.

Chicory Vinaigrette

¼ cup vinegar
1 tablespoon blueberry blossom honey
1 teaspoon kosher salt
½ teaspoon pepper
2 tablespoons gourmet espresso syrup
2 shallots, finely diced
1 teaspoon chopped parsley
½ cup pecan oil

Place the vinegar, honey, salt, pepper, syrup, shallots, and parsley in a medium bowl and stir to combine. Slowly drizzle the pecan oil in a steady stream while whisking vigorously with a wire whip. Check the seasoning.

To assemble the brown sugar–cured diver scallops with chili-pecan dressing and chicory vinaigrette: Place an equal portion of dressing on each of four plates, top with two scallops, and drizzle with chicory vinaigrette.

BUFFALO OSSO BUCCO WITH MOLASSES SWEET POTATOES, CARAMELIZED PEACHES, BOURBON DEMI-GLACÉ, AND CARAMEL "HAY"

Pork Osso Bucco

Salt and pepper
1 cup flour
4 large meaty pork shanks, about 1¼ pounds each, about 3-inch lengths
4 teaspoons Creole seasoning
¼ cup olive oil
4 tablespoons butter
4 large carrots, diced

2 large onions, diced

4 stalks celery, diced

12 cloves garlic

½ cup bourbon (Buffalo Trace)

2 bay leaves

1 gallon beef or veal stock or brown chicken stock

4 orange slices, ¼ inch thick

1 Add salt and pepper (to taste) to the flour. Season the shanks with the Creole seasoning and dust them with the seasoned flour. Shake off excess flour. Preheat the oven to 350 degrees. Using a heavy-gauge ovenproof pot or covered roasting pan, heat the oil and butter over high heat on the stovetop until very hot and sear the shanks until they have a good crust and are very nicely browned. Turn them over and sear until a crust appears again, about 5 minutes. Remove from the pan and set aside.

2 Add the carrots, onions, celery, and garlic to the pan and cover and cook them until browned, about 10–12 minutes, stirring every few minutes. Pour off the excess fat and add the pork shanks back to the pan. Deglaze with the bourbon and cook for 1 minute. Add the bay leaves and stock. Place 1 orange slice on top of each shank, bring the mixture to a boil, and cover and place the roasting pan in the oven. Roast for approximately 3 hours, until very tender, checking occasionally to make sure the liquid doesn't cook away; add more stock or water if needed. Gently remove the shanks from the pot; set aside and keep warm by wrapping in foil.

3 Strain the braising liquid into another container and skim off whatever fat rises to the top. Return it to the stove and bring it to a boil, skimming away any fat that comes to the top. Cook the sauce until it can coat the back of a spoon. Add a splash of your favorite bourbon and a pat of butter and check the seasoning.

Molasses Whipped Sweet Potatoes

3 large sweet potatoes, about 1 pound each
¼ cup molasses
¼ cup honey
  Kosher salt
  White pepper
4 tablespoons butter
½ teaspoon cinnamon
⅛ teaspoon grated nutmeg

Preheat the oven to 350 degrees. Peel and quarter the sweet potatoes and put them in a roasting pan. Pour in 1 cup of water, drizzle the sweet potatoes with the molasses and honey, and season with the salt and pepper. Cover the pan with a tight-fitting lid or aluminum foil and bake for about 1 hour. Remove the cover and continue cooking for another 30 minutes, until the potatoes are dark brown and very tender. Remove them to the large bowl of an electric mixer, add the butter, cinnamon, and nutmeg, and mix until all the lumps are gone. Pour in as much of the cooking liquid as desired, continue whipping for another minute, check consistency and seasoning (you can add more honey, molasses, or butter if desired), put the potatoes in a large casserole dish, and serve immediately.

Caramelized Peaches

2 peaches, cut in half and peeled
2 tablespoons turbinado sugar
½ cup bourbon

Press the peaches cut side down into the turbinado sugar. In a heavy-gauge sauté pan, heat the peaches until very hot. Place them cut side up and cook 5 minutes, until the sugar is well caramelized; it should have a golden-brown color. Turn the peaches over, add the bourbon to the pan, cover, and continue cooking several minutes, until peaches are quite soft. Remove the peaches and add the remaining liquid to the pork braising liquid (the sauce to be drizzled over the pork).

Caramel Hay

1   cup water
1   cup sugar

Put the water and sugar in a small sauce pan and bring to a boil over medium heat. As the water evaporates, the sugar will start to collect on the sides of the pan. Using a pastry brush, wipe some water on the sides to clean away collected sugar, but *do not stir*. Continue cooking until the sugar is cooked to the hard crack stage, remove the pan from heat, and let it cool slightly. When almost cool, dip a fork into the caramelized sugar and shake the fork back and forth over the handle of a wooden spoon, creating finely spun "hay." Let the hay cool and place it in an airtight container or serve it immediately.

To assemble the buffalo osso buco with molasses sweet potatoes, caramelized peaches, bourbon demi-glacé, and caramel hay: Place equal amounts of sweet potatoes on four plates, place one shank on top of each, drizzle with sauce, and garnish with one peach half and caramel hay.

....

Dark Chocolate Bread Pudding Soufflé

Bread Pudding

- ¾ cup sugar
- 1 teaspoon cinnamon
- ⅛ teaspoon nutmeg
- 3 eggs
- 1 cup heavy cream
- 2 ounces semisweet chocolate, melted but not hot
- 1 teaspoon vanilla extract
- 5 cups 1-inch cubes of stale French bread

Bourbon Sauce

- 2 teaspoons cornstarch
- 2 teaspoons water
- 1½ cups heavy cream
- ⅓ cup sugar
- ½ cup bourbon

Meringue

- ¾ cup sugar
- ½ cup cocoa powder
- 9 egg whites
- ¼ teaspoon cream of tartar

1 *To make the bread pudding*: Preheat the oven to 350 degrees. Combine the sugar, cinnamon, nutmeg, and eggs in a large bowl and beat with an electric mixer until smooth. Slowly pour the cream into the warm chocolate and then pour this mixture into the egg mixture. Add the vanilla and bread cubes and mix well, allowing the bread to soak up the liquid. Lightly grease a 9 × 13-inch pan, pour the mixture into it, and place it in the oven. Bake the pudding for 30 minutes, until it is golden brown and firm to the touch. Let it cool to room temperature.

2   *To make the bourbon sauce*: Make a slurry by mixing the cornstarch and water until smooth. Bring the cream to a boil in a small saucepan over medium heat. Add the cornstarch slurry to the cream and return it to a boil, stirring constantly. Add the sugar and bourbon and stir until the sugar dissolves. Remove the sauce from the heat and cover it with a lid to keep it warm.

3   *To make the meringue*: Mix the sugar and cocoa powder together. Bring the egg whites to room temperature in a large bowl and add the cream of tartar to them. Beat with an electric mixer until the mixture is foamy. Gradually add the sugar mixture and continue whipping until the mixture is shiny and thick. Do not overwhip, or the egg whites will break down and the soufflé will not work.

4   Preheat the oven to 350 degrees and lightly butter six 5-to-6-ounce ramekins. Break the bread pudding into small pieces and place them in a medium bowl. Add one-fourth of the meringue to the bowl and gently mix, trying not to lose the air in the meringue. Place equal portions into the ramekins. Top each ramekin with some of the remaining meringue, and using a spoon, smooth and shape the top into a dome over the ramekin rim. Immediately place the soufflés in the oven and bake for 15–20 minutes or until they begin to brown. Serve immediately with the warm sauce. (At the Bourbon House they like to poke a hole into the soufflé and pour the sauce into the soufflé at the table.)

NOTES

ONE BEVERAGES

1 Jackson, *Whiskey*, 14.
2 Anderson, *A Love Affair with Southern Cooking*, 342.
3 Standage, *A History of the World in 6 Glasses*, 122–23.
4 Fussell, *The Story of Corn*, 263.
5 Schmid, *The Hospitality Manager's Guide to Wines, Beers, and Spirits*, 17.
6 Anderson, *A Love Affair with Southern Cooking*, 342. Bourbon County, Kentucky, is not the only place in North America named for the former royal family of France. Kansas also has a Bourbon County, and Indiana and Missouri, two states that both used to produce bourbon whiskey, have townships named Bourbon. There is also Fort Bourbon in Canada on the north shore of the Saskatchewan River; and New Orleans is known for Bourbon Street. Standage, *A History of the World in 6 Glasses*, 126.
7 Anderson, *A Love Affair with Southern Cooking*, 342.
8 Curtis, *And a Bottle of Rum*, 9.
9 Dornenburg and Page, *What to Drink with What You Eat*, 277.
10 Flexner, *Out of Kentucky Kitchens*, 22.
11 Wondrich, *Esquire Drinks*, 50.
12 DeGroff, *The Essential Cocktail*, 159.
13 Flexner, *Out of Kentucky Kitchens*, 41.
14 Koskela, *The New Orleans Bartender*, 5.
15 Hoge, *The Bourbon Cookbook*, 273.
16 Mautone, *Raising the Bar*, 158.
17 Wondrich, *Imbibe!* 237–38.
18 DeGroff, *The Craft of the Cocktail*, 138.
19 Biggs, *Cocktail Classics*, 70.
20 Wondrich, *Imbibe!* 197.
21 Lipinski and Lipinski, *Professional Beverage Management*, 437.
22 Wondrich, *Esquire Drinks*, 51.
23 Tsutsumi, *101 Great Tropical Drinks*, 14.

24 Nickell, *The Kentucky Mint Julep*, 43.

25 Claiborne, *Craig Claiborne's Southern Cooking*, 346, 345.

26 Perhaps the most notable Kentucky Colonel was Colonel Harland Sanders of Kentucky Fried Chicken (KFC) fame. "The Colonel" used his honorary title to market his secret recipe and took on the role of a southern colonel although during his military service he never rose above the rank of private. Other famous Kentucky Colonels include Pope John Paul II, Hunter S. Thompson, Ashley Judd, General Omar Bradley, Sir Winston Churchill, and Muhammad Ali.

27 Honorable Order of Kentucky Colonels, http://kycolonels.org.

28 Martin and Brennan, *In the Land of Cocktails*, 69.

TWO WINTER

1 Miller, *Secrets of Louisville Chefs Cookbook*, volume 2 (2005), 113.

2 Greenberg, *Gourmet Cooking with Old Crow*, 114.

3 Todd, *Taste of Indianapolis*, 72.

4 Anderson, *A Love Affair with Southern Cooking*, 84.

5 Miller, *Secrets of Louisville Chefs* (2003), 60.

6 Warren, *The Art of Southern Cooking*, 227.

7 Miller, *Secrets of Louisville Chefs* (2003), 80.

8 Allison-Lewis, *Kentucky's Best*, 185.

9 Fearing, *Southwest Cuisine*, 202–4.

THREE SPRING

1 *Splendor in the Bluegrass*, 107.

2 Ibid., 116.

3 Fearing, *Southwest Cuisine*, 215.

4 Flexner, *Out of Kentucky Kitchens*, 257–58.

5 Ibid., 194.

FOUR SUMMER

1 Labensky and Hause, *On Cooking*, 443.

2 Lee and Lee, *The Lee Bros. Southern Cookbook*, 336–38.

3 *Southern Living 1988 Annual Recipes*, 129.

4 Belk, *Around the Southern Table*, 235–36.

5 Kingsford Products Company, *Kingsford America's Best BBQ*, 20.

6 *Southern Living 1987 Annual Recipes*, 139.

FIVE FALL

1 Tolley and Mitchamore, *Jack Daniel's the Spirit of Tennessee Cookbook*, 38.

2 Today, Jack Daniel's is owned by the Brown-Forman Corporation in Louisville.

3 Lundy, *Shuck Beans, Stack Cakes, and Honest Fried Chicken*, 135–37; Anderson County Burgoo Festival, "The Burgoo Song," www.kentuckyburgoo.com/.

4 Joachim, *A Man, a Can, a Grill*, 41.

5 *Splendor in the Bluegrass*, 185.

6 Greenberg and Greenberg, *Whiskey in the Kitchen*, 166.

7 Roux, *Fried Coffee and Jellied Bourbon*, 36.

8 Hoge, *The Bourbon Cookbook*, 263.

9 Ibid., 106.

10 *Southern Living 1987 Annual Recipes*, 264.

11 Hayes, *Cooking with Heart and Soul*, 197–98; Corriher, *CookWise*, 125.

12 *Southern Living 1988 Annual Recipes*, 236.

GLOSSARY

ANISETTE A generic name for an anise-and-licorice-flavored liqueur, also known as anis.

APPLEJACK American brandy distilled from apple wine; also known as apple brandy.

AQUA VITAE Latin for "water of life"; sometimes still used to refer to distilled beverages.

BARBECUE A method of cooking food (mostly meat) with gas, coals, or wood and the use of a rub, a marinade, or a sauce.

BITTERS Distilled spirits containing an infusion of a natural bittering compound, such as herbs, roots, or barks; also known as a digestive aid because bitters tend to soothe and relax the stomach. Bitters are among the original ingredients used to make a cocktail, along with a spirit (whiskey, rum, etc.), sugar, and water.

BOURBON An American whisk(e)y made predominantly from corn under specific guidelines, including the use of new oak barrels.

BEURRE BLANC An emulsified white butter sauce made with butter, white wine reduction, and shallots and usually served with seafood.

CARAMELIZE Cook sugar until it begins to brown. Sugar of one kind or another is found in many foods and will cause browning as the food cooks.

COCKTAIL A class of alcoholic beverage in which a distilled spirit is mixed with other flavorings such as juice, fruit, or soda to make the final beverage before it is served. Originally a beverage was considered a cocktail only if it contained a spirit, sugar, water, and bitters.

COINTREAU A premium, brand-name, triple sec or orange-flavored liqueur made from bitter oranges. Cointreau orange liqueur was first sold by brothers Adolphe and Edouard-Jean Cointreau in 1875.

COUNTRY HAM A salt-cured ham that may or may not be hardwood-smoked. Also known as Virginia ham.

DEGLAZE Remove the cooked-on bits at the bottom of a pan with the addition of liquid.

EAU DE VIE French for "water of life"; generally refers to grape brandies.

FLAME   Burn off alcohol by lighting with a match. Also referred to as flaming and flambé and used in both tableside cooking and drink presentation. *Caution*: when flaming any alcoholic beverage, be careful to always tip the pan away from you.

GROG   Originally a drink of rum and water named for Admiral Edward Vernon. Admiral Vernon required his men to drink the mixture every day to ward off scurvy. His men called the admiral "Old Grog" because of his coat made from grogram, a coarse fabric woven from wool and silk. The admiral also lends his name to the Washington family residence, Mount Vernon. American sailors were routinely served grog until September 1, 1862.

HARD CRACK STAGE   A description of sugar that has become hard by being heated to 295–310 degrees and then cooled.

MADEIRA   A fortified wine made on the island of Madeira. The wine is fortified with brandy, so that the alcohol content is increased to between 17 percent and 20 percent by volume. The five styles of Madeira, from sweetest to driest, are Malmsey, Bual, Rainwater, Verdelho, and Sercial.

MINT   An herb that is used in many recipes because it lends a cool, sweet, fresh, aromatic flavor to the final dish. There are twenty-five species and various hybrids of mint.

MUDDLER   A small, hand-held, batlike instrument used for crushing ice, fruit, cube sugar, fresh mint leaves, or other herbs.

PERNOD   A brand of anise-flavored liqueur made by Pernod-Ricard, a French company that produces many alcoholic beverages, including Four Roses bourbon.

PROHIBITION   The period between 1920 and 1933, when the production, sale, and transportation of alcohol was illegal. Prohibition began with the Eighteenth Amendment to the U.S. Constitution and ended with the Twenty-first Amendment.

REDUCE   Concentrate a liquid by simmering and allowing the water to evaporate.

RYE   Whiskey made from at least 51 percent rye grain. This is a unique product that is not Canadian or American blended whiskey, which tends to be substituted at most bars when patrons ask for rye. Rye is also known as rye malt whiskey.

SHERRY   A fortified wine from Spain, sherry comes in two basic categories, fino and oloroso. Sherry is traditionally served with the soup course.

SIMPLE SYRUP   A sugar syrup made from equal parts sugar and water and boiled together for 3 minutes to stabilize the sugar in an invert or liquid form.

SLOE GIN   A red liqueur made from sloe berries or blackthorn berries, which give it a tart plum flavor. This liqueur is not made from gin.

SLURRY   A mixture of equal parts cornstarch and water that is used to thicken sauces.

SOFTBALL STAGE   A description of sugar that is heated to 234-45 degrees and then cooled. It has a soft consistency that will ball. This cooked sugar is used in fudge.

SUPERFINE SUGAR (CASTOR SUGAR)   A fine grade of granulated sugar that is used both in the bakery and in the bar because it dissolves into the final product better than regular granulated sugar. Also known as baker's sugar or bar sugar.

SWEAT   Heat in a pan over low-heat so as to cook without adding color to the food.

TODDY   A mixed drink containing a distilled spirit, sugar, water, and spices. Toddies are usually served hot.

UISCE BEATHA   Gaelic for "water of life."

USICE BEATHA   Irish for "water of life."

VERMOUTH   A fortified, spiced wine used in many cocktails.

VOLSTEAD ACT   This is another name for the Eighteenth Amendment to the U.S. Constitution, which made illegal the production, sale, and transportation of alcohol.

WHISKEY   A distilled spirit made from grain that has been aged in oak barrels. Whiskey, spelled with the *e*, refers to either Irish or American whiskeys.

WHISKEY REBELLION   The 1794 rebellion of farmers against the U.S. Government over a new tax on whiskey imposed by Congress at the urging of Alexander Hamilton, the secretary of the treasury. The incident was quickly resolved when President George Washington led thirteen thousand to fifteen thousand troops in a show of force of the new federal government.

WHISKY   A distilled spirit made from grain that has been aged in oak barrels. Whisky, spelled without an *e*, refers to either Scotch whisky or Canadian whisky but can also refer to some American whiskeys.

BIBLIOGRAPHY

Allison-Lewis, Linda. *Kentucky's Best: Fifty Years of Great Recipes*. Lexington: University Press of Kentucky, 1998.

Anderson, Jean. *A Love Affair with Southern Cooking*. New York: HarperCollins, 2007.

Belk, Sarah. *Around the Southern Table*. New York: Simon & Schuster, 1991.

Biggs, David. *Cocktail Classics*. London: Connaught, 2004.

Cecil, Sam K. *The Evolution of the Bourbon Whiskey Industry in Kentucky*. Paducah, KY: Turner, 1999.

Claiborne, Craig. *Craig Claiborne's Southern Cooking*. New York: Clamshell Productions, 1987.

Corriher, Shirley. *CookWise: The Hows and Whys of Successful Cooking*. New York: William Morrow, 1997.

Curtis, Wayne. *And a Bottle of Rum: A History of the New World in Ten Cocktails*. New York: Crown, 2006.

Deen, Paula, with Melissa Clark. *Paula Deen's the Deen Family Cookbook*. New York: Simon & Schuster, 2009.

DeGroff, Dale. *The Craft of the Cocktail*. New York: Clarkson Potter, 2002.

———. *The Essential Cocktail*. New York: Clarkson Potter, 2008.

Dornenburg, Andrew, and Karen Page. *What to Drink with What You Eat*. New York: Bulfinch Press, 2006.

Fearing, Dean. *Southwest Cuisine: Blending Asia and the Americas*. New York: Grove-Weidenfeld, 1990.

Flexner, Marion. *Out of Kentucky Kitchens*. Lexington: University Press of Kentucky, 1989.

Fussell, Betty. *The Story of Corn: The Myths and History, the Culture and Agriculture, the Art and Science of America's Quintessential Crop*. New York: Knopf, 1992.

Greenberg, Emanuel. *Gourmet Cooking with Old Crow*. Frankfort, KY: Old Crow Distillery, 1970.

Greenberg, Emanuel, and Madeline Greenberg. *Whiskey in the Kitchen*. New York: Bobbs-Merrill, 1968.

Hall, Michael C., Liz Sharples, Richard Mitchell, Niki Macionis, and Brock Cambourne. *Food Tourism around the World: Development, Management, and Markets*. Burlington, MA: Butterworth-Heinemann, 2003.

Hawkins, Nancy, and Arthur Hawkins. *The American Regional Cookbook*. Englewood Cliffs, NJ: Prentice Hall, 1976.

Hayes, Isaac. *Cooking with Heart and Soul*. New York: Putnam's, 2000.

Hoge, Tom. *The Bourbon Cookbook*. Harrisburg, PA: Stackpole Books, 1975.

Jackson, Jeremy. *The Cornbread Book: A Love Story with Recipes*. New York: HarperCollins, 2003.

Jackson, Michael. *Whiskey: The Definitive World Guide*. New York: DK, 2005.

Joachim, David. *A Man, a Can, a Grill: 50 No Sweat Meals You Can Fire Up Fast*. Rodale, 2003.

Kingsford Products Company. *Kingsford America's Best BBQ*. Publications International, 1993.

Koskela, Sean. *The New Orleans Bartender*. Harahan, LA: Express, 2001.

Labensky, Sarah, and Alan Hause. *On Cooking: A Textbook of Culinary Fundamentals*. 3rd ed. Upper Saddle River, NJ: Prentice Hall, 2003.

Lee, Matt, and Ted Lee. *The Lee Bros. Southern Cookbook*. New York: Norton, 2006.

Lipinski, Bob, and Kathie Lipinski. *Professional Beverage Management*. New York: Wiley, 1996.

Lundy, Ronni. *Shuck Beans, Stack Cakes, and Honest Fried Chicken: The Heart and Soul of Southern Country Kitchens; Seasoned with Memories and Melodies from Country Music Stars*. New York: Atlantic Monthly Press, 1991.

Martin, Ti Adelaide, and Lally Brennan. *In the Land of Cocktails: Recipes and Adventures from the Cocktail Chicks*. New York: HarperCollins, 2007.

Mautone, Nick. *Raising the Bar: Better Drinks Better Entertainment*. New York: Artisan, 2004.

Miller, Nancy. *Secrets of Louisville Chefs*. Louisville: Tobe, 2003.

——. *Secrets of Louisville Chefs Cookbook, Volume 2*. Louisville: Louisville Magazine, 2005.

Nickell, Joe. *The Kentucky Mint Julep*. Lexington: University Press of Kentucky, 2003.

Old Bardstown Bourbon Cookbook. Bardstown, KY: Willett Distilling, 1967.

Roux, Willan C. *Fried Coffee and Jellied Bourbon: A Culinary Guide Book for Autocrats of the Breakfast Table, Containing Reliable Recipes and Cooking Instructions*. Barre, MA: Barre, 1967.

Schmid, Albert. *The Hospitality Manager's Guide to Wines, Beers, and Spirits*. 2nd ed. Upper Saddle River, NJ: Prentice Hall/Pearson Education, 2008.

Southern Living 1987 Annual Recipes. Birmingham, AL: Oxmoor House, 1987.

Southern Living 1988 Annual Recipes. Birmingham, AL: Oxmoor House, 1988.

Splendor in the Bluegrass. Louisville: Junior League of Louisville, 2000.

Standage, Tom. *A History of the World in 6 Glasses*. New York: Walker, 2005.

Todd, Joan S. *Taste of Indianapolis: Recipes from the City's Best Restaurant Kitchens.* Indianapolis: Emmis, 1996.

Tolley, Lynne, and Pat Mitchamore. *Jack Daniel's the Spirit of Tennessee Cookbook.* Nashville, TN: Rutledge Hill Press, 1988.

Tschumi, Gabriel. *Royal Chef: Recollections of Life in Royal Households from Queen Victoria to Queen Mary.* London: William Kimber, 1954.

Tsutsumi, Cheryl Chee. *101 Great Tropical Drinks: Cocktails, Coolers, Coffees, and Virgin Drinks.* Waipahu, HI: Island Heritage, 2006.

Warren, Mildred Evans. *The Art of Southern Cooking.* New York: Gramercy Books, 2003.

Willis, Virginia. *Bon Appétit, Y'all: Recipes and Stories from Three Generations of Southern Cooking.* Berkeley, CA: Ten Speed Press, 2008.

Wondrich, David. *Esquire Drinks: An Opinionated and Irreverent Guide to Drinking.* New York: Hearst Books, 2002.

——. *Imbibe! From Absinthe Cocktail to Whiskey Smash: A Salute in Stories and Drinks to "Professor" Jerry Thomas, Pioneer of the American Bar.* New York: Penguin, 2007.

BOURBON

DISTILLERIES IN KENTUCKY

Buffalo Trace Distillery
1001 Wilkinson Boulevard
Franklin County, Kentucky
502-696-5926
800-654-8471
www.buffalotrace.com

Four Roses Distillery, LLC
1224 Bonds Mill Road
Lawrenceburg, Kentucky
502-839-3436
www.fourroses.us

Heaven Hill Distilleries Bourbon Heritage Center
1311 Gilkey Run Road
Bardstown, Kentucky
502-337-1000
www.bourbonheritagecenter.com
www.heavenhill.com
funfolks@bourbonheritagecenter.com

Historic Tom Moore Distillery
300 Barton Road
Bardstown, Kentucky 40004
502-348-3774

Jim Beam Distilling Company
149 Happy Hollow Road
Clermont, Kentucky
502-543-9877
www.jimbeam.com

Makers Mark Distillery
3350 Burks Springs Road
Loretto, Kentucky
270-865-2099
www.makersmark.com

Wild Turkey Bourbon
Austin, Nichols Distilling Company
U.S. Highway 62 East
Lawrenceburg, Kentucky
502-839-4544
www.wildturkeybourbon.com

Woodford Reserve Distillery
7855 McCracken Pike
Versailles, Kentucky 40383
859-879-1812
www.woodfordreserve.com

NAME AND SUBJECT INDEX

RECIPE INDEX